# GRAND ACTIVITIES

## More Than 150 Fabulous Fun Activities For Kids To Do With Their Grandparents

*Shari Sasser*

**Career Press**
*Franklin Lakes, New Jersey*

GRAND ACTIVITIES
Cover design by Shari Sasser
Printed in the U.S.A. by Book-mart Press

To order this title, please call toll-free 1-800-CAREER-
1 (NJ and Canada: 201-848-0310) to order using VISA
or MasterCard, or for further informa-tion on books
from Career Press.

The Career Press, Inc., 3 Tice Rd., P.O. Box 687,
Franklin Lakes, NJ 07417

**Library of Congress Cataloging-in-Publication Data**

Sasser, Shari.
Grand activities : more than 150 fabulous fun activities for
kidsto do with their grandparents / Shari Sasser.
    p.    cm.
ISBN 1-56414-427-5 (pbk.)
    1. Grandparent and child.   2. Child rearing.
    3. Creative activities and seat work.   I. Title
HQ759.9.S3         1999
306.874'5--dc21                          99-41527

To my beautiful grandmothers,
Lee & Eleanor,
*who blessed my life*
*and inspired this book*

# Contents

# Contents

## GROWING BY LEAPS & BOUNDS

## CALENDAR EVENTS

## SACRED CELEBRATIONS

## JUST BECAUSE I LOVE YOU

## SPECIAL REQUESTS

# INTRODUCTION

• • • • • • • • • • • • • • • • •

**M**y sisters and I were very lucky little girls. Growing up, we had a home full of wonderful people: four of us girls, two loving parents and Gramma. Yes, Gramma. In today's world, families may be separated by many miles. Many children today seldom see their grandparents. Yet we had our Gramma under the same roof. I do not even think we knew how lucky we were. Looking back, I can see how much we touched each other's lives. My grandmother helped to mold us all into the ladies we are today. We gave her laughter and love.

In today's busy world, everyone has less time. Ours is a fast-paced world of high technology in which computers answer our phones, microwaves cook our meals, and mail is electronic. Children today rarely grow up to find jobs in their hometown or live in close proximity to their parents. *Grand Activities* serves as the medium by which grandchildren and grandparents can stay connected with each other in a very special, personal way, no matter how far apart they live apart.

This book is filled with activities: drawing, writing, cooking, videotaping, and computer activities to name just a few. These activities are designed to provoke thought and capture the personalities of a grandchild and his grandparent. Many of the activities take only minutes to do. Most of the activities result in finished pieces to be sent, given to and enjoyed by a grandparent. All of the activities serve to strengthen the bond between grandparent and grandchild.

I have included activities that are easy to do, but your child may need assistance for some. You will find the bond between you and your child grow stronger, too, as you help him or her. For your convenience, the time requirement, supplies and goals for each activity are listed on the side of each page. The materials you will need vary for each activity, but most are things you have around the house already. None of the materials are expensive or hard to find.

It is my sincere desire that this book will help your family build and maintain precious bonds. You will be amazed at how such simple activities can bring so much joy into the lives of your children and their grandparents.

*Shari Sasser*

# FIRST THINGS FIRST

# WELCOME TO THE CLUB

**Materials Needed**
imagination

**Time Required**
30 minutes to set up the club, few minutes occasionally to conduct "club business"

**In The End**
Grandparent and grandchild will have established a special bond

## OTHER IDEAS

~

Let your child create a banner for the club and identification badges for the members

Your child and his grandparent share a very special bond. Throughout their lives that bond will strengthen, and the activities in this book will help them to create special memories together.

Encourage your child to begin a special "club" with his grandparent. Its membership is restricted to only them, (and maybe siblings), and they can talk to each other to establish their own rules and regulations. They can invent the following things for their exclusive club:

- Club name
- Secret Word or Phrase
- Club Motto
- "Meeting" Times
- Secret Handshake
- Secret Code Names
- Club Goals
- Official Rules

By creating the club, the two will have set the foundation for years of fun and special bonding.

# BULLETIN BOARD

• • • • • • • • • • • • • • • • • • • •

Through the years, your child will accumulate many cards and letters from her grandparent. Rather than just reading each card or letter and tossing it aside, encourage your child to keep each one in a place where it can be seen and appreciated for more than the amount of time it takes simply to read it.

Purchase an inexpensive corkboard and some clips and thumbtacks. Let your child paint the board or glue ribbons around the edges. She can attach sequins or pom-poms, noodles or shells around the borders.

Once finished, the bulletin board can be put up in her room in a visible location. The correspondence she receives from her grandparent can be displayed on it throughout the years, updated from time to time as necessary.

This special bulletin board will be a visible reminder that your child has a grandparent who loves her.

**Materials Needed**
corkboard, paints, ribbon, assorted decorative items

**Time Required**
45 minutes

**In The End**
Child will create a special place to display letters from Grandparent

## OTHER IDEAS

~

Purchase a cork sheet that can be rolled and packed in a shipping container. Have your child decorate it and send it to her grandparent to display cards and letters from the child.

# FABULOUS FOLDER

● ● ● ● ● ● ● ● ● ● ● ● ● ● ● ● ● ● ●

**Materials Needed**
butcher paper, tape or stapler, crayons, markers, paint

**Time Required**
30 minutes

**In The End**
Child will create a folder in which to store items he receives from his grandparent

## OTHER IDEAS

~

Have your child make a folder for his grandparent to store all of the wonderful artwork and letters he will be receiving from your child. It can be folded and mailed to the grandparent.

A grandparent's job is to spoil a child. That means lots of letters, cards, pictures and gifts will be accumulated by your child through the years. It would be a shame to simply discard these items after they are enjoyed for only a short time.

After displaying correspondence from his grandparent on a bulletin board for some time, your child will need a place to store all of these items for his future enjoyment. Let him make a big folder for this purpose.

Simply purchase a roll of butcher paper or plain brown packing paper. Unroll it, cut off two yards of it and fold it in half to create a rectangle one yard long. Tape or staple around the bottom and side edges, leaving the top open to create a huge folder.

Let your child decorate the folder with paint, crayons or markers. When finished, the folder can be stored in a closet or slid under a bed or dresser. It will be a handy place to keep all of the things he receives from his grandparent that it would be a shame to throw away.

# DAY TO DAY

# COMIC RELIEF

Materials
Needed
ruler, pencil or
pen

Time Required
20 minutes

In The End
Grandparent will
have a comical
look at a day in
the life of his
grandchild

Most people's days contain a little of everything. Good and bad. Happy and sad. Exciting and dull. Easy and hard. This is a fairly common truth, and we can see it reflected in the daily newspaper.

Toward the back of each day's newspaper, we can always find the comic page. It is there to make us laugh. No matter what kind of day we have, it is important to tackle it with a sense of humor. We should be able to think of several funny or amusing things that happen each day.

Using a ruler as a guide, instruct your child to draw a rectangle about 3 inches tall and 9 inches wide. Draw two vertical lines to divide the strip into three equal sections, or frames, each 3 inches wide. These are the frames for her own comic strip.

## OTHER IDEAS

Have your child create an original comic character with a personality based on that of her grand-parent. She can invent funny situations for the character and create comic strips all about her grandparent.

Clip your child's favorite comic strip out of the newspaper to share with her grandparent.

Help your child remember something funny that happened today, and have her illustrate the event in a series of three drawings that show just how it happened. Include speech bubbles to hold the words of communication between characters, and captions along the top or bottom if more explanation is needed.

Send the finished strip to your child's grandparent for some real comic relief.

# TODAY'S NEWS

• • • • • • • • • • • • • • • • • •

**W**atching the daily newscast on television with your child can be a very educational experience. What better way to catch up on events on a worldwide and local level in just a matter of minutes? Some networks even have special news segments or entire broadcasts just for kids.

Let your child do a live broadcast of the news of her day. Have her write down important (or not so important) events in the following categories:

> **Headlines**
>
> **World News**
>
> **Local News**
>
> **Breaking News**
>
> **Weather**
>
> **Sports**

Encourage her to dress up like an anchorperson on the news. You can even paper clip a "pretend microphone" to her clothes. Have her sit up straight behind a table with her notes in front of her. Explain that she should try to only glance at her notes occasionally and keep her eyes on the camera as much as possible. Then let the camcorder go to work!

Record her newscast and send it to her grandparent for a welcome alternative to the real news of the world.

**Materials Needed**
pen, paper, dress-up clothes, camcorder & videotape

**Time Required**
30 minutes

**In The End**
Grandparent will be able to see the daily news through the eyes of her grandchild

## OTHER IDEAS

Have your child do large drawings to illustrate each news story. The pictures can be held up to simulate graphics on the real newscast.

Let siblings help to do funny commercials between the different categories of news.

# MAKING THE GRADE

**Materials Needed**
access to copy machine, red pen

**Time Required**
10 minutes

**In The End**
Grandparent will see how much his grandchild is learning

**R**eport card day can be a good day, or not so good day. But it is always the moment of truth. Inevitably, there will be some surprises - mostly for the parents. Most kids know pretty much what the numbers will say.

Many schools require a parent's signature on the report card to ensure that it has been seen. The next time a report card comes home, make a photocopy of it before sending it back to school. Have your child think about each and every grade on it.

Give him a red pen, and let your child make comments alongside each grade. Suggest that he address such questions as whether or not he is proud of that grade. Was it hard to achieve? Could he have done better? What can he do to improve next time? Does he enjoy that class and why?

Send the report card to his grandparent who will be proud to share in the achievement of the grades. No doubt, he will also be glad to read the words of wisdom added to the report card by his goal-setting grandchild.

## OTHER IDEAS

Let your child do a report card on his teachers. Have him comment on how effectively they teach and interact with the students and on what they can do to be better teachers.

Pretend that your child is the teacher. What kind of a report card would he do for a student like himself?

# DREAM NETS

* * * * * * * * * * * * * *

We all dream each night, but we do not always remember our dreams. Those that we do remember are often strange and hard to understand. They can be wonderful or frightening.

Children can often verbalize and visualize their dreams better than adults can. Their descriptions can be quite detailed.

The next time your child tells you about a dream, encourage her to "capture" her dream on paper, like capturing a butterfly in a net. Like a butterfly, memories of dreams can be vivid and beautiful and flutter away in an instant.

Provide some paper and pencils, crayons or markers and have her draw pictures of what she can remember about her dream. Because dreams are mostly visual, the picture is the most important part of this activity.

Captions can be added, or a whole narrative can be written to accompany the picture and provide explanation.

Send this dream report to your child's grandparent and let her see how fascinating is the mind of her grandchild.

**Materials Needed**
paper, pencils, crayons, markers

**Time Required**
15 minutes

**In The End**
Grandparent will share a glimpse of her grandchild's imagination

## OTHER IDEAS

Help your child to expand her understanding of her dream by asking her about whether she would like to have that same dream again or what she thinks the dream meant.

Suggest your child keep a dream journal of drawings and written descriptions to refer to when she needs an idea for a creative writing project.

# A STILL LIFE

● ● ● ● ● ● ● ● ● ● ● ● ●

**Materials Needed**
pencil, paper, crayons, markers, or watercolors

**Time Required**
30 minutes

**In The End**
Grandparent will enjoy a work of art portraying items that are precious to his grandchild

## OTHER IDEAS

@

Arrange several groups of favorite items in different places in the house and use a camera to photograph them instead of drawing them. After the photos are developed, be sure to write captions on the back before sending them.

One of the most basic kinds of paintings that artists undertake is the still life. It's practical purpose is to study the visual relationship between objects and to capture their three-dimensional image realistically on a two-dimensional surface like paper or canvas. It is a lesson in light and dark, shadow and color. The subject being drawn or painted is likely an arrangement of fruit or flowers.

Your child can create a still life of a more playful nature. Let him select a few of his favorite things, trying to choose items that hold some sort of significance to him. It is preferable that they differ in shape, size and color. Arrange them on a table, dresser or bed. The items should be arranged in a close group, overlapping and leaning on each other. This arranging of parts will create a unified "composition" that will be the subject of the still life.

Using a pencil first, your child can slowly start to sketch the composition onto his paper. The more closely he looks at the items, the easier it will be to draw them. He should not hesitate to use the eraser as much as needed! When everything is sketched in place, colored pencils, crayons or watercolors can be used to add color to the piece.

The end result will be a work of art even better than those of master artists. Your child's grandparent will love to receive it in the mail and will appreciate it more than an antique painting. After all, it contains items that are precious to the most precious artist in the world.

# THE YEAR IN REVIEW

• • • • • • • • • • • • • • • • • • • • • • •

Time flies, and before you know it, another school year has come and gone. The end of the year is so exciting; cleaning out lockers, bringing home supplies, saying goodbye to homework for the summer.

Although events of the year seem so clear that they will never be forgotten, take some measures to guarantee that they will always be remembered.

Throughout the school year, have your child create an informal and fun list of short comments to include:

| | |
|---|---|
| Favorite Subject | Worst Subject |
| Nicest Teacher | Meanest Teacher |
| Best Friend | Best Book Read |
| Proudest Moment | Funniest Moment |
| Fondest Memory | Worst Cafeteria Food |
| Most Challenging Project | |
| Most Embarrassing Moment | |
| Important Lessons Learned | |

Place the list in a folder with pockets and fill the pockets with report cards, graded papers, art projects, and class photos. Don't forget tickets to sporting events, programs from musical performances, menus from the cafeteria and awards for achievement.

Label the folder with the grade number and year and send it away to the child's grandparent at the end of the year.

Materials Needed
paper, pen, folder with pockets, memorabilia

Time Required
a few minutes scattered throughout the course of the school year

In The End
Grandparent will have a keepsake of an entire year in the life of her grandchild

OTHER IDEAS

Make a photocopy of the "yearbook" contents for your child to keep. She can write descriptive captions on the copied sheets, capturing memories for years to come. Include "secret notes" from friends and personal momentos in her own folder.

# LIGHTS! CAMERA! ACTION!

**Materials Needed**
camcorder, videotape

**Time Required**
30 minutes

**In The End**
Grandparent will be entertained by grandchild

## OTHER IDEAS

Videotape a puppet show starring puppets made from socks or brown paper lunch bags.

Include "Coming Attractions" at the end of the performance to hint at future taped shows, perhaps sequels to the original.

If your child tends to be a "ham," and puts on little plays or concerts for you at home, seize the opportunity to pick up the camcorder and capture the moment on film for her grandparent.

If no spontaneous performance has happened lately, suggest that your child plan a presentation specifically for this purpose. She will love getting props together and dressing up for her play. She can write a script or improvise, use a spoon and pretend it's a microphone for a singing concert or act out some scenes from a favorite story. Leave the planning of it completely up to the child and enjoy the final performance.

The taped show or concert will bring such joy to your child's grandparent and will likely be infinitely better than any regularly scheduled programming on television.

# MY PERSONAL PILLOW

H as your child grown out of one of his favorite shirts? Maybe it's a night shirt or pajama top, soccer jersey or gymnastics leotard. Perhaps a painting smock or dress shirt. Kids grow so quickly, it seems that no sooner than a shirt is declared to be a favorite, it is already too small to wear.

You can turn that little shirt into a fun pillow in just minutes, and your child can have a lesson in sewing. Thread the embroidery needle with thread and show your child how to do a simple running stitch (in and out, in and out, as shown below).

Sew the head and arm openings shut and then insert the foam rubber, batting or old pillow into the shirt from the bottom. When the shirt is rather plump and full of the stuffing, sew the bottom opening shut. The result is a nice large pillow that will be fun for your child's grandparent to toss onto her bed or couch.

**Materials Needed**
old shirt, needle & thread, foam rubber, batting or old pillow

**Time Required**
1 hour

**In The End**
Grandparent will receive a unique pillow to display as a daily reminder of her grandchild

## OTHER IDEAS

Decorate the shirt with paint pens or glue sequins, pom-poms or patches onto the shirt to add even more personality.

Create coordinating pillows from old shorts or cut-off jeans or create a life-size "grandchild pillow" by sewing shirt and pants pillows together, creating a head out of a stuffed piece of fabric.

# IT'S A TIE!

**Materials Needed**
old tie, sequins, beads, T-shirt paint, thread, glue and scissors

**Time Required**
35 minutes

**In The End**
Grandparent will sport a tie made specially for him by his grandchild

## OTHER IDEAS

For a special touch, paint words on the tie, such as "Happy Birthday" or "I Love My Grandson."

Apply comic strip characters to the tie. Simply glue them on, then apply a mixture of glue and water with a paintbrush, which will create a clear glaze over the picture once it is dry.

These days, both men and women are wearing ties. For men, it is a traditional dressy look; for women, a casual and fun fashion statement. Let your child decorate a fun tie for his grandparent.

Select an old tie that is no longer being worn by anyone in your home. If you don't have one, you can easily and inexpensively purchase one at your local thrift store. It does not matter whether the tie is a solid color or covered with a pattern.

Provide sequins, beads, T-shirt paint and embroidery thread and watch your child's creativity run wild. Let him paint, sew, glue and cut. He can enhance the current pattern on the tie or paint over it and create a pattern of his own.

When finished and completely dry, the tie will slip nicely into a large envelope to be sent to your child's grandparent. It will certainly become a favorite accessory in his or her wardrobe.

# GRIN & BEAR IT

· · · · · · · · · · · · · · · · · · ·

Almost every child has a favorite "friend." It may be a stuffed puppy, bunny or doll, but often it is a teddy bear. Teddy bears are special because they are always there to "listen" to problems and provide company, love and comfort.

Yet when it is time for formal photographs, the faithful teddy bear is often left out. Be sure to include the bear in some photos so that he will be remembered long after he is needed on a daily basis. Have a photo session just for him!

Let your child dress the bear in different outfits, hats or jewelry and take his picture in various locations around the house or yard. After the pictures are developed, glue or tape them to a piece of construction paper or insert them into a removable page from a photo album. Let your child write captions for each photo.

When finished, have a color copy of the page made that you can send to your child's grandparent. Keep the original for your child to refer to when she is older. She will be glad to have this photo memory of her old best friend.

**Materials Needed**
camera & film

**Time Required**
20 minutes

**In The End**
Grandparent will get to know his grandchild's favorite "friend"

## OTHER IDEAS

Let some other stuffed animals or dolls participate in the photo session and pose with the teddy bear.

Place cut-out paper "speech bubbles" on the photo to contain the bear's comments.

# GOOD MEASURE

**Materials Needed**
ruler, pen & paper

**Time Required**
15 minutes

**In The End**
Grandparent and grandchild will get to compare many elements of their homes and bodies

## OTHER IDEAS

**Measure in centimeters**

**Use a tape measure to determine how far it is from bedroom to bathroom, kitchen to living room, etc.**

Learning how to use a ruler is not only an important exercise, it is a lot of fun. Here's a way to have your child learn proficiency at that skill while having fun and learning more about his grandparent, too.

Provide your child with a ruler and instruct him to measure and record the length of the following things:

| | |
|---|---|
| body height | little finger |
| strand of hair | foot from toe to heel |
| arm | leg |
| bed | couch |
| dining room table | refrigerator |
| car | height of desk chair |
| dog or cat | bedroom dimensions |

Add or subtract from the above list as desired, and send a copy of the list to the child's grandparent. The grandparent, in turn, should measure the same items at her house and send the measurements back to the child.

In this way, they can compare and contrast their own size and the size of many things around both of their homes.

# HOME SWEET HOME

F lowers and well pruned bushes do not make a house a home. Only the love of the people who live there can make this happen. A home should be a place of comfort and safety, love and laughter. To see what makes a house a home, you must look on the inside.

Let your child create a picture of your house with doors and windows that open to reveal the people inside. Have her draw the house on a piece of paper. Try to fill the entire page with the facade of the house, making it as large as possible. Cut around the doors and windows, leaving them attached on one of the sides to create a flap that can fold back.

Lay the drawing over a piece of paper of the same size and open all of the flaps. Lightly trace around the openings onto the paper below to leave little frames in which to draw the family. Lift off the top drawing and fill each door or window frame on the lower paper with a member of the family. Color both pictures, apply glue to the back of the top picture and place it onto the bottom one, being careful to align all of the doors and windows properly.

The end result is a picture of your home with functioning doors and windows through which to view your whole family. After receiving the picture, your child's grandparent will almost feel like he is there!

**Materials Needed**
construction paper, scissors, glue

**Time Required**
45 minutes

**In The End**
Grandparent will see his grandchild's home even if he is far away

## OTHER IDEAS

Don't forget to include your pets in the picture. Pets are "people," too!

Add some activity to the outside of your picture, such as the mailman or neighbors passing by.

# MEAL APPEAL

● ● ● ● ● ● ● ● ● ● ● ● ● ● ● ●

## Materials Needed
plastic utensils, paper plates, napkins, construction paper, markers

## Time Required
20 minutes

## In The End
Child will create "silverware," plates and napkins for grandparent to use

## OTHER IDEAS

Enclose a short summary of what your child did throughout the day today in the package with the place setting. This way, her grandparent can almost feel like he was part of the dinner table conversation!

**M**eal times are special family times. It is nice when the whole family can share meals together and talk about events of the day. Despite the fact that your child's grandparent may not be able to join you for meals as often as you would all like, there is an easy way for your child to be a special part of his grandparent's meals.

Purchase a box of plastic utensils, paper plates and napkins and some permanent waterproof markers. Let your child decorate the plates, napkins and handles of the utensils with the markers. She can do any kind of decorative motif. Encourage her to give some thought to his designs. Perhaps she can draw designs that mimic the pattern of dinnerware she uses at home. Perhaps she can choose funny or loving words or phrases or names of his favorite meals. Maybe she would like to draw stars, swirls, triangles or hearts. The possibilities are endless.

To complete the setting, let your child decorate a tabloid size sheet of construction paper to create a place mat. You can cut little fringes along the edges, if desired.

Place the table setting in a box or large mailing envelope and wrap it up to be mailed. Include a little note from your child about the fact that while they may not eat all their meals together, this special place setting will serve as a reminder of the special bond between grandchild and grandparent.

# KEEPING TIME

● ● ● ● ● ● ● ● ● ● ● ● ● ● ● ● ●

**M**ost of our lives are run on a schedule. Our family generally wakes up, works and eats meals around the same time every day. Work and school days are clocked to the minute, and each task, class and event is assigned a time.

Have your child and his grandparent exchange copies of their daily schedules. This way, they can have a better understanding of what a typical day holds for each other. Remind your child to include the time that he wakes up, the time that he goes to sleep, and everything in between from math class to recess, lunch to supper.

Materials
Needed
pen & paper
Time Required
10 minutes

In The End
Grandparent
and grandchild
learn about
each other's
daily schedules

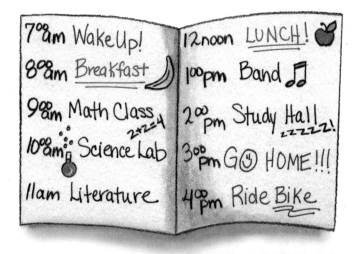

7⁰⁰am Wake Up!
8⁰⁰am Breakfast
9⁰⁰am Math Class
2+2=4
10⁰⁰am Science Lab
11am Literature

12noon LUNCH!
1⁰⁰pm Band ♪♫
2⁰⁰pm Study Hall zzzzz!
3⁰⁰pm GO HOME!!!
4⁰⁰pm Ride Bike

They can each write highlights of the other's schedule on a small business card-size piece of paper that will be easy to carry in a pocket. This way, when your child needs a quick pick-me-up in the middle of the day, he can check and see what his grandparent is doing at that time, and his grandparent can do the same thing when he needs a moment of joy in his day.

Encourage your child to learn about different time zones. If his grandparent lives in a different time zone than he does, take that into consideration when determining exactly what each other are doing at any given time.

## OTHER IDEAS

Have your child make a clock out of a paper plate, labeling each number with the activity his grandparent is doing at that time. The hands of the clock can be attached in the center of the clock with a metal brad or fastener so that they can be moved around as desired.

# A DAY IN MY LIFE

**Materials Needed**
disposable camera, pen

**Time Required**
a few minutes throughout the course of a day

**In The End**
Grandparent will be able to see what her grandchild does during an average day

School days are such exciting days in your child's life. He is making friends and learning a lot. If your child has "Open House" night at school and gets to show off his work and classrooms, his grandparent may not be able to attend.

There are things at school that would be really neat for grandparents to see. Here is a way to share all of that.

After obtaining his teachers' permission, (teachers may think of a way to make this a part of a school project!), allow your child to bring a disposable camera to school one day. Tell him to take pictures of all of his classrooms, his locker or cubby, the gym, playground, even the bathroom! Have him photograph special science equipment of interest or murals on the walls and get photos of friends and teachers.

Get the pictures developed and then have your child write descriptions on the backs of them. Put the photos in the mail to his grandparent. This way, she can see what it is your child does every day. She can see what the school looks like and what kind of special features it has. Best of all, she will feel more a part of her grandchild's everyday life—a feeling not every grandparent gets the privilege to have.

## OTHER IDEAS

Get double prints made of the pictures. Mount one set in a notebook and write captions for each photo. Let your child bring it to school for show and tell.

Assemble color copies of the photos and cut and paste them into a collage or arrange them in a multiple frame.

# GREAT GIFTS TO GIVE

# A "T" FROM ME

**Materials Needed**
T-shirt, fabric paint, (varied other materials depending on method you choose)

**Time Required**
45 minutes

**In The End**
Grandparent will receive a T-shirt made specially for him by his grandchild

# OTHER IDEAS

Decorate a handkerchief or pair of socks with one of the methods described.

Let your child make a matching shirt for himself.

L et's face it, everyone loves to wear a T-shirts. They are the perfect choice for comfort and relaxation. T-shirts are very inexpensive to buy, and fun to decorate for people you love. Here are some fun ways to decorate a T-shirt for your grandparent:

- **Fish Print** – Use a real fish, maybe one your child caught himself! Dry the fish with a paper towel and lay it on a stack of newspaper. Paint it with a thin coat of fabric paint. Press the T-shirt onto it and then carefully peel it back off. After the paint dries, use little tubes of squeeze fabric paint to apply more detail, if desired.

- **Tie-Dye** – Gather the shirt in little bunches all around and fasten the bunches tightly with rubber bands. Dip the "tied up" shirt in fabric dye according to package directions. Allow to dry for half of the drying time. Remove the rubber bands and dry completely.

- **Marbled** – Scrunch up an old rag and dip it in fabric paint. Dab most of the paint off onto a piece of newspaper, leaving only a small amount on the rag. Apply paint to the shirt by blotting the rag all around, overlapping slightly so that the entire surface of the shirt is eventually "marbled."

- **Message** – Paint a simple message on the shirt. Maybe something like, "I ☼ My Granddaughter" or "Smile!"

- **Dazzling** – Sew large sequins onto the shirt. Arrange them in floral patterns, or create a random design.

# WRAP IT UP

• • • • • • • • • • • • •

**D**espite the large selection of colorful wrapping paper that exists in stores, none compare to homemade wrap. There are many different ways to create original wrapping paper.

One technique is to create a "printing press" to distribute designs onto the paper. Simply cut some shapes out of felt or cardboard and glue them all around the outside of an empty oatmeal box or juice can.

Pour a very thin layer of paint onto a paper plate and roll the press (the box or can) through it, coating the shapes with paint. Next, roll the press over the paper and watch the painted shapes appear on the wrapping paper. When the color fades, roll the press through the paint again. Continue this technique until all of the paper is covered with shapes.

Have your child consider using letters instead of shapes. He could spell his name or that of his grandparent. Maybe he could create a phrase like, "For You" or "With Love."

Allow the paint to dry, and roll up the paper until the next time your child has a gift to send to his grandparent. Any present wrapped in this handmade paper will almost be too pretty to unwrap.

## Materials Needed
felt or corrugated board, empty oatmeal box or juice can, glue, scissors, poster paint, white butcher paper

## Time Required
30 minutes

## In The End
Grandchild will create handmade wrapping paper to use for gifts to grandparent

# OTHER IDEAS

★

Make matching gift cards in the same shapes that you used to decorate the paper.

★

Try different textures or shapes by using the ridged side of corrugated board, corduroy or other fabrics to make the shapes.

# CREATIVE CANDLES

**Materials Needed**
cotton string, paraffin, coffee can, crayon shavings, paint brush, water

**Time Required**
1 hour

**In The End**
Grandchild will create decorated candles for grandparent

## OTHER IDEAS

★

Place flower petals on the candle, then "paint" over them with melted paraffin to seal them onto the candle. When the paraffin dries, it will be fairly clear and the petals will show through beautifully.

★

Decorate store-bought candles if you do not have time to make your own.

For more than 3,000 years, candles have been used to bring light into dark places. In modern times, they are used more as decoration than as necessity, and they are popular gift items.

Candles are inexpensive to buy, but are very simple and fun to make. Use a piece of cotton string about 12" long for the wick. Melt some paraffin in an empty coffee can in a double boiler. A double boiler must be used, as paraffin catches fire easily if overheated. Fill another coffee can with cold water.

Dip the wick into the paraffin, then into the cold water. Continue to dip back and forth until the candle is the width you want it to be. You can dip only one end of the wick, or dip both ends, holding the wick in the center. The latter method will produce two hanging candles connected by a wick. The wick can later be cut so the candles can be used, or the candles can be hung on a hook for display.

To decorate the candles, grate some old crayons with a cheese grater or chop them up with a knife or chopper. Melt the shavings in a coffee can in a double boiler and let your child use the colorful melted wax as "paint" to add decoration to the candles. Have him paint designs, personal phrases or messages specially for his grandparent. When the candles are dry, send them to your child's grandparent.

# MARVELOUS MATS

• • • • • • • • • • • • • • • • • • • •

L et's face it, much of our daily life takes place in the kitchen. It is a meeting place and feeding place. It is the one room in the house where people seem drawn to gather and talk. Even when not in use, the kitchen table is a main focal point in the kitchen. The table should reflect the personality of its owner and look inviting. Placemats are a good way to display personality and color on the kitchen table. They can be functional or merely decorative.

Here are some simple ways your child can create eye-catching placemats for her grandparent.

- **Weaving** – Use an 11" x 17" piece of construction paper and cut parallel straight lines at 1" intervals all the way across

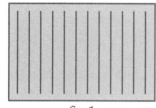

*fig. 1*

it, stopping 1/2" from the edge on both sides. (See *fig. 1*) Cut 10 strips of construction paper to be 17" long and 1"wide. Weave the strips in and out of the slits cut in the big paper to create a woven mat. Cover mat with a sheet of clear contact paper.

- **Leaves and Flowers** – Sandwich assorted leaves and flowers between two sheets of wax paper and put them between the pages of a heavy book for several days. Remove them and arrange them on the sticky side of an 11" x 17" piece of clear contact paper. Carefully lay another piece of contact paper on top, sticky side down to create a clear mat decorated with natural flora.

- **Hand Prints** – Let your child cover his hands with paint and cover an 11" x 17" piece of construction paper with hand prints of all colors. When prints are dry, cover the mat with clear contact paper.

**Materials Needed**
construction paper, scissors, clear contact paper, leaves and flowers, washable poster paint

**Time Required**
30 minutes

**In The End**
Grandparent's meals will be enhanced by eating off of placemats made by his grandchild

## OTHER IDEAS

★

Have your child write personal messages on paper napkins. The napkins will work with the placemats to brighten her grandparent's meals.

# NIFTY NAPKIN RINGS

## Materials Needed
paper towel or toilet tissue rolls, colored construction paper, tape or glue, clear spray paint or polyurethane glaze

## Time Required
45 minutes

## In The End
Grandparent will be able to decorate his table with napkin rings designed especially for him

## OTHER IDEAS

★

Use markers to decorate a set of paper napkins to coordinate with the napkin rings.

★

Instead of paper shapes, wrap colorful yarn around and around the rings to create softer, more formal-looking napkin rings.

Not every table is adorned with a set of napkin rings. Many people think it is too fancy for their lifestyle. Here is an easy way to create a set of very casual napkin rings that your child's grandparent can use every day.

Cut an empty paper towel or toilet tissue roll into 1 1/2" sections to create eight rings. Then, cut some colored construction paper into eight strips that are 1 1/2" wide and 6" long. Wrap one strip around each ring and secure it with tape or glue.

Next, create decorative shapes out of construction paper and glue them onto the rings. Your shapes can be abstract and decorative or follow a specific theme. For example, do floral rings for the spring, orange and yellow leaves for the fall, different kinds of athletic balls for a grandfather who loves sports or a variety of colorful butterflies for a grandmother who loves nature.

When the glue is dry, take the rings outside and lay them on a stack of newspaper to spray them with clear spray paint or polyurethane glaze. After they are dry, pack them carefully in a shoebox and send them to a lucky grandparent.

# CAN DO!

● ● ● ● ● ● ● ●

These rustic looking candle holders are meaningful gifts and look great in a windowsill or sitting outside on the doorstep as a welcome to visitors.

Clean an empty can, any size, and remove its paper label. Fill it almost to the top with water and put it in the freezer until it the water is frozen. Once frozen, bring it to your work surface and put it on a stack of newspaper or folded towels.

Using a hammer, tap a large nail into the can until it pierces the metal. Pull out the nail, move it over and do it again, creating a pattern or design with the punched holes.

After the design is complete, set the can in the sink to let the ice melt and carefully dry the can with a paper towel. Place a votive candle in it and there you have it! Send the candleholder to your child's grandparent and have your child include a note stating that his grandparent is a great "light in his life" and instructing the grandparent to use the candle to brighten his day.

**Materials Needed**
aluminum can, hammer, large nail, votive candle

**Time Required**
30 minutes, after water is frozen

**In The End**
Child will create a candleholder for his grandparent

## OTHER IDEAS

Do not freeze water in the can. Instead, use a can opener to create a row of triangular shapes along the top and bottom of the can. Do this with strict adult supervision, as the metal will be sharp.

Create a series of candle cans, either all the same size or all different sizes, to be displayed together.

# DECOUPAGE DESIGNS

Materials
Needed
old magazines,
scissors, glue,
water, paint-
brush, shoe box

Time Required
45 minutes

In The End
Grandparent will
receive a box that
can be used to
collect letters
from his grandchild

## OTHER IDEAS

Use pictures
from wrapping
paper or
favorite birth-
day or holiday
cards.

Instead of
pictures, use
colored tissue
paper or dried
leaves and
flower petals
to cover
the box.

The technique of decorating a surface with paper cutouts is called decoupage. It is a simple technique that can be used to decorate everything from picture frames to jewelry boxes.

Have your child decoupage a shoe box in which to send his next shipment to his grandparent. The grandparent can then use the box to store and organize photos, recipes, letters from his grandchild or other momentos.

The first step is to cut out magazine pictures that are appealing because of their content or are just nice to look at.

Pour a small amount of water into a plastic bowl and slowly add white glue, stirring constantly until the mixture is a soupy consistency. Use a paintbrush to spread some of the mixture onto a small area of the box and apply the cutouts to that area, overlapping the pictures to cover the box completely. Add more glue mixture to another area and continue in this fashion until the entire box is covered with pictures.

Apply a thin coat of the glue mixture over the entire box to seal the pictures in permanently and to create a clear glaze when dry. Allow the box to dry completely before using it or mailing it to the grandparent.

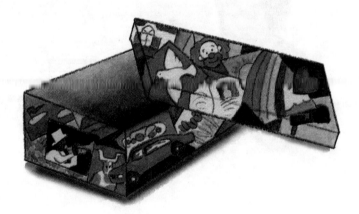

# LANTERN LIGHTS

• • • • • • • • • • • • • • • • • •

A plain votive candle and a mayonnaise jar can be transformed into a lantern that, when a candle is burning inside, will glow and shed a beautiful, colorful light. This activity uses these two ordinary items to create a beautiful eye-catching gift for your child's grandparent.

Clean an empty mayonnaise jar and soak it in warm water for ten minutes. While it is still wet, remove the label — it should peel right off. Dry the jar completely.

Make a mixture of glue and water that is a soupy consistency. Using a paintbrush, apply glue to the outside of the jar and cover it with white tissue paper. When it is completely covered, brush a thin layer of the "glue soup" all over it.

Next, apply small squares of colorful tissue paper all over the jar, overlapping or not to create the kind of look you desire. If you want to, you can cut specific shapes out of the tissue — stars, flowers, swirls or stripes. Again, paint over the entire thing with glue soup, which will dry to create a clear coating. When finished and dry, it is a beautiful lantern that, when sent to your child's grandparent, will fill her home with a warm, colorful light.

**Materials Needed**
votive candle, empty mayonnaise jar, glue, paintbrush, colored tissue paper

**Time Required**
40 minutes

**In The End**
Grandchild will create a lovely lantern for her grandparent

## OTHER IDEAS

Sprinkle glitter onto the white tissue instead of, or in addition to, the colored tissue paper.

Allow the white tissue layer to dry completely. Then, instead of applying the colorful tissue, use markers to decorate the jar.

Wrap a wire around the top of the jar to hang it.

# SPICY SHAPES

● ● ● ● ● ● ● ● ● ● ● ● ● ● ●

**Materials Needed**
cinnamon, apple-sauce, rolling pin, cookie cutters

**Time Required**
35 minutes

**In The End**
Grandchild will create pleasant-smelling ornaments for grandparent

# OTHER IDEAS

★

Omit the holes in some of the shapes. These can be placed in drawers as air fresheners or glued to magnets to be used on the refrigerator.

✻

Tie three of the shapes together on one ribbon and designate that group to hang from the rearview mirror of your child's grandparent's car.

**O**f all the smells of the kitchen, few are as comforting as the smell of fresh cinnamon. Maybe because cinnamon reminds us of apple pie or hot cider, pumpkin bread or snickerdoodles.

Here's a recipe for a cinnamon dough that is intended to enjoy, but not to eat. Mix 1 1/2 cups of cinnamon with one cup of applesauce. That's it! Combine it very well to form a dough.

The dough can be rolled out and cut into shapes with cookie cutters. Once that is done, use a skewer to poke a hole through the top of each shape. Wiggle the skewer around until the hole is large enough to pass a ribbon through it.

Place the shapes on a piece of stiff cardboard and put them in a warm place to dry. The top of the refrigerator is perfect. They should be completely dry in a few days, especially if you flip them over every once in awhile to let air circulate.

Once finished, tie ribbons through the holes of each shape for hanging. The shapes are delicate, but will last for years, (and continue to smell like cinnamon) if they are treated with care. Pack some up and send them to your grandparent who can hang them in a closet or anywhere else that a soft clean aroma is desired.

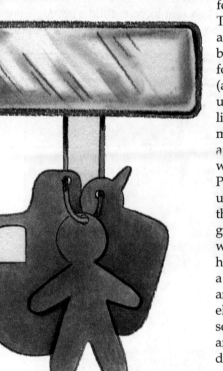

# GOOD CLEAN FUN

Decorative soaps add a very nice touch to any bathroom and make the person who uses them feel very special. Your child can create some adorable little soaps to add joy—and cleanliness—to his grandparent's day.

To make your own decorative soaps, mix two to four cups of soap flakes with 1/2 to one cup of water. Whip the two with an electric mixer, adding flakes or water as needed to achieve a mixture the consistency of cookie dough.

The soap "dough" can be sculpted by hand to make any shape imaginable from snowmen to sailboats. The dough can also be rolled out and cut with cookie cutters or molded in cookie or candy molds.

After shaping the dough by any method mentioned (or any other way you can think of), allow the soaps to dry on wax paper and then wrap them in tissue paper and send them to your child's grandparent.

**NOTE:** Another fun way to create little soaps is simply to melt glycerin and pour it into ice cube trays that have been lightly sprayed with cooking oil spray. For a fun twist, drop a bead, coin, figurine or other tiny treasure into each section of the tray before the glycerin hardens. The grandparent will be able to see it through the soap and look forward to using the soap every day to get it to melt down enough to release the little "prize."

**Materials Needed**
Soap flakes, water, electric mixer, cookie cutters, cookie or candy molds, glycerine, ice cube trays

**Time Required**
45 minutes

**In The End**
Grandparent will have fun soaps to remind her of her grandchild

## OTHER IDEAS

After your soaps are dry, use a toothpick to carve details in them. For example, you can add eyes and buttons to a snowman or indicate veins on the leaves of a flower.

Carve a bar of commercially bought soap carefully with a paring knife and a toothpick.

# MAGNETIC ATTRACTION

**Materials Needed**
magnetic tape, small toys and other miscellaneous trinkets

**Time Required**
20 minutes

**In The End**
Grandparent will receive adorable magnets to display on her refrigerator

## OTHER IDEAS

★

Paint some small rocks and glue wiggle eyes on them to create little creatures — they make adorable magnets.

★

Gather shells the next time you are at the beach and make them into magnets.

Refrigerators were invented to keep food cold, but that is not all that they do. Most refrigerators double as art and photo galleries, becoming virtually covered with photographs of loved ones and artwork of children.

Magnetic tape is easily found at most discount or hardware stores and can transform almost anything into an attractive homemade magnet. Purchase the kind with one sticky side and then begin selecting items to magnetize!

Small toys that are no longer played with, groups of little crayons tied together with yarn or wallet-size photos in tiny frames make wonderful magnets. Cardboard cutouts of stars sprinkled with glitter, pom-poms transformed into

fuzzy animals and artificial flowers work wonderfully, too. Dog biscuits coated with clear glaze make clever magnets to hold photos of pets, and tickets from sporting events make great magnets for sports lovers.

Simply adhere magnetic tape to the back of the items after removing the paper covering the sticky tape side. If the item you have selected is not flat on the back, it is better to use glue to attach the item to the magnet rather than using the sticky tape. Magnets are available in almost any shape and size if you determine that the magnetic tape is not the best choice for you.

Your child's grandparent will be thrilled to receive these creative magnets and will put them to good use.

# FRUITY HOT PADS

. . . . . . . . . . . . . . . . . . . . .

**E**ven if your child can't be there with his grandparent, he can still help her in the kitchen. Creating an original hot pad is one way to be a part of the daily work of cooking.

Make a "sandwich" with layers in the following order: piece of brightly colored felt, sheet of polyester batting, another piece of felt.

Draw a large fruit shape on the top piece of felt and cut out the shape, cutting through all three pieces of fabric at once.

Glue or sew the pieces together around the edges and decorate them with felt leaves, stems, and seeds.

Send the hot pads to the child's grandparent who will certainly appreciate the extra help in the kitchen.

**Materials Needed**
felt, polyester batting, scissors, glue or needle and thread

**Time Required**
40 minutes

**In The End**
Grandchild will create hot pads for his grandparent

## OTHER IDEAS

Create floral, fish, leaf or other shapes instead of fruit.

# PAPER PRESENTS

● ● ● ● ● ● ● ● ● ● ● ● ● ● ● ● ● ● ● ●

**Materials Needed**
paper, colored tissue paper, glue, paintbrush

**Time Required**
45 minutes

**In The End**
Child will create handmade stationery for his grandparent to use

## OTHER IDEAS

★

Paint your child's fingers or some shapely leaves, then stamp them around the border of the stationery to decorate it with finger-prints or leaf shapes.

★

Try using lit-tle circles left by a hole punch! Glue them in place around the border of the stationery.

**M**any holidays throughout the year are associated with gift giving. It is sometimes hard to think of something personal to give for every Mother's Day, Father's Day, birthday, etc. We always want to give a thoughtful gift that will be liked and used.

Try letting your child present his grandparent with a gift of homemade stationery for the next holiday. Get a stack of typing paper and cut it all in half to create a nice size stationery. Get some tissue paper in various colors and cut it into 1/4" squares. Dilute some glue with water and, using a paint brush, have your child apply glue around the border of a piece of the paper. He should then place squares of tissue all around the border of the paper, overlapping colors if desired. Instruct him to do this for every sheet of stationery he wants to make.

When the glue is very dry, close the pieces of stationery between the pages of a heavy book. Stack some more heavy books on top of it and wait for a few days. When you remove the sta-tionery from the book, it will be nice and flat.

A gift of stationery is one that will be greatly appreci-ated. Now, when your child's grandparent writes letters to her friends to brag about her grand-child, she can do it on paper that he decorated just for her.

# FRIENDSHIP PINS

I t is nice to have something special with you at all times that serves as a reminder that you are loved. Friendship pins are just perfect for the job! Small and unobtrusive, these little colorful pins will brighten the day of your special grandparent each time she glances at them.

Buy some colorful beads at the craft store. The ones that work best for this activity are tiny plastic beads just barely larger than candy sprinkles that you would put on cupcakes. They come in little packs that should cost less than a dollar, and one little pack contains hundreds of beads!

Pour the beads into a bowl and supply your child with several safety pins. He can thread the beads onto the pins, leaving enough pin at the point to be able to close it again.

The finished pins can be put in an envelope with a little note to his grandparent, explaining the sentiment of love that is held in each little pin. They can be worn on shirt pockets, ties or zippers of jackets. The most fun place to put them is on shoelaces, where pins of assorted colors and sizes can be collected.

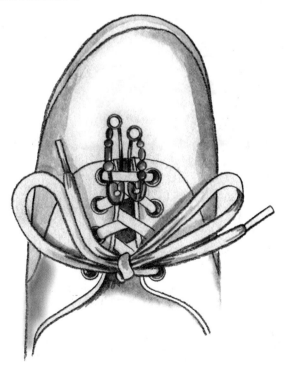

**Materials Needed**
safety pins, tiny plastic beads

**Time Required**
15 minutes

**In The End**
Grandchild makes little friendship pins for grandparent

# OTHER IDEAS

★

Thread some little charms onto the pins in addition to the beads for an added touch.

★

Let your child make matching pins for himself as special unifying tokens between his grandparent and himself. When they both have a set of the same ones, they can remember each other every time they glance at them.

# A YEAR WITH YOUR DEAR

**Materials Needed**
calendar, glue, scissors, magazines, photos

**Time Required**
1 hour

**In The End**
Grandparent will have a daily reminder of her loving grandchild

## OTHER IDEAS

★

Have your child mark special dates on the calendar with markers or stickers.

**E**ach year, as the New Year approaches, people's thoughts turn to the future. We make resolutions and set goals for the upcoming year.

New calendars become available in stores to prepare us for the new year but almost every household receives at least one calendar for free, whether it be from a bank, from a charitable organization, or another place of business.

Those free calendars usually have nice photographs for each month, but you can make them very personal. Take that calendar and help your child turn it into a very special gift for her grandparent.

Cut twelve pieces of colored construction paper to the same size as the pictures of the calendar. Glue the paper over the pictures. Now comes the creative part. Have your child create an original work of art on each month's colored paper. Let her use crayons, markers, stickers, glue and glitter, chalk and ink stamps. You may use pictures she did in the past or pictures from magazines, too. Let her be imaginative and apply comic strips or word puzzles, candy wrappers or snips of wrapping paper. Best of all, have her glue on some pictures of herself and your family.

When the calendar is complete, send it to her grandparent with a note that says "Happy New Year," which it really will be, because every day on the calendar will be a reminder of a wonderful grandchild.

# OUR FAMILY HISTORY

# HOW WE GOT HERE

**Materials Needed**
family documents, parent's brain, history book, encyclopedia or Internet access

**Time Required**
2 hours

**In The End**
Grandchild will learn about his roots

## OTHER IDEAS

~

Assume the role of one of your ancestors and write a short story about your life.

America is often referred to as a melting pot because its people come from so many different places and have joined together to form one unified country. This is something to be proud of, and it is interesting to learn about our own family's history and origin.

Learning more about her own family's history will perhaps help your child to gain a better understanding of her grandparent. It will certainly build an awareness of the factors and influences that made your family what it is today.

Have your child gather as much information as possible about the previous generations in your family. Tell her everything you know about the subject and consult old family documents, photos and records. If your ancestors were from another country, strive to gain an understanding about the factors that motivated them to move to America. If your family has been in the same town for generations, learn about their impact on that town and their ties to it.

Encourage your child to take notes about the information she discovers. After learning about your own family's history, consult a history book, encyclopedia or the Internet to learn about the country of your ancestors. What was it like? What kind of government ruled it? What were its main crops or industries? What was going on during the years that your family left?

Have your child write "Family History" at the top of a piece of paper and fill the page with the most interesting facts she learned. Send a copy to her grandparent who will appreciate the effort and share the pride in your family.

# ¡HOLA, ABUELA!

Children around the world use different words to describe their grandparents. Even here in the United States, children call their grandparents a variety of names to include Grandma & Grandpa, Granny & Papa, Grandmama & Grandaddy, Ganny & Gampy and many more.

Encourage your child to ask their friends at school what they call their grandparents. Have them research different languages and heritages to learn as many nicknames for grandparents as possible. For example, Jewish children may choose the Yiddish names of Bubbe and Zayda for their grandmother and grandfather. Different cultures have their own traditions, as do different families.

Your child can form a list of the names that are discovered. Beside each name, note the culture, family or language that uses it.

Send a copy of your child's findings to his grandparent with an explanation that no matter what she is called, she is the best grandparent in the world.

To create a visual illustration of his findings, your child can write the name that his grandparent goes by in large, block letters on a piece of paper. In small letters, fill up the blocks with the many world-wide grandparent names.

**Materials Needed**
pen & paper

**Time Required**
1 hour total

**In The End**
Grandparent will compare his name to those of many other grandparents around the world

## OTHER IDEAS

~

Learn different words for "granddaughter" and "grandson," "son" and "daughter."

~

Let your child pretend she is a grandparent and decide which name she will want to go by. It can be one that already exists, or one that is made up.

# EGG HEADS

· · · · · · · · · · · · · ·

**Materials Needed**
egg shells, markers, cotton balls, potting soil, alfalfa or grass seeds

**Time Required**
15 minutes initially, then a minute a day for a while

**In The End**
Grandparent will enjoy seeing her likeness in this new medium

**H**ere is a fun way to create a family portrait unlike any you have created before. Although they may only loosely resemble your family members, these egg heads will certainly bring smiles to their faces.

Carefully crack open some eggs. Save the eggs in a bowl in the refrigerator for tomorrow's breakfast. It is the shells you will need for this activity. Gently wash them with warm soapy water and allow them to dry.

Let your child use markers to draw faces on the shells and transform each one into a member of your family. Be sure to do this with the open, or cracked side up, like a little bowl. Use the larger shells for the larger family members. Take the shape of each shell into consideration when choosing which one to use for each person.

Turn an empty egg carton upside down and rest each "egg head" between the ridges to hold them in an upright position. Fluff out some cotton balls to make them as large and airy as possible and place one in each egg head. Sprinkle each with a little soil and then with alfalfa or grass seeds.

Place the "family" on a window sill or countertop and moisten them daily with water. Before long, they should each have "hair" sprouting from their head. Watch it grow each day, pruning back the hair of family members with short hair and letting those with long hair grow and grow.

The end result is a hilarious family of green-haired egg heads. Take a photograph of them to send to your grandparent. Be sure to label it with each person's name. Your grandparent has likely never been honored by having her family portrait done "in egg."

# OUR FAMILY CREST

Years ago, families of several cultures were identified by emblems that were designed to represent their family. Some of these family crests were worn on shields of the men in the family when they went to battle. Some of them were made into flags. Family crests are seldom used today.

It is fun to think about what your family's crest would look like. Have your child design a crest for your family.

First, brainstorm about the things that your family stands for: occupations that have been held for generations, religious background, traditions and culture. Sketch out symbols that represent these things and then devise a way to incorporate some of those symbols into a single, visually interesting design.

Photocopy the family crest down to a height of about two inches. Cut out the little crest and glue it to a piece of paper, centering it in the middle about 1/2" from the top. Write your family's last name beneath it with a black pen. Photocopy that paper onto some parchment colored paper to create family stationery.

Your child's grandparent will love to receive and use the thoughtful, very personal gift of stationery.

## Materials Needed
paper, pen, parchment paper, access to copy machine

## Time Required
1 hour

## In The End
Grandparent will have personalized family stationery

## OTHER IDEAS

~

Have your child make a crest for his maternal grandparent using his mother's maiden name.

~

Scan the crest into your computer and print it out onto self-adhesive labels to be used on envelopes to match the stationery.

# COMFY GENES

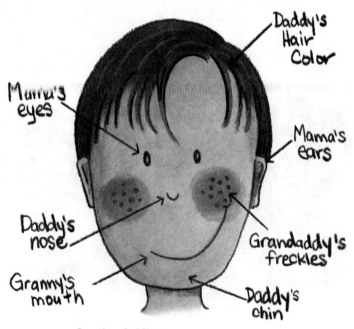

**Materials Needed**
photos, mirror, pencil, paper

**Time Required**
20 minutes

**In The End**
Child will try to determine which of his parents or grandparents influenced his physical traits

## OTHER IDEAS

~

Make a list of traits other than facial features and note where they may have originated. Things like artistic skill, physical prowess, mathematical brilliance and scientific interest may be traits that were handed down by parents or grandparents.

Genetics is the study of heredity and exactly how a person comes to inherit different traits from his parents. Each person is a mixture of his mother and father and has a unique "recipe" made of very specific "ingredients" from each parent.

Almost immediately after birth, a child is described as "having his mother's eyes" or being the "spittin' image of his father." Some traits may skip a generation, appearing in a child and his grandparent, but not in the child's parent. These are the traits that are most pleasing to the grandparents!

Have your child gather a photo of each of his parents and grandparents and then sit in front of a mirror with a pencil and paper. Let him study each feature of his face, noticing its shape, size and color. Have him draw his face or glue a photo of himself in the center of a piece of paper and then draw a line pointing from each feature out to the paper where he should specify where he thinks the gene for that particular feature came from. For example, "Gramma's eyes" or "Papa's ears."

Send the drawing to your child's grandparent, who may be surprised to see that every feature on the child did not necessarily come from her.

Daddy's Hair Color

Mama's eyes

Mama's ears

Daddy's nose

Grandaddy's freckles

Granny's mouth

Daddy's chin

# PAPER PEOPLE

It is normal for members in a family to have disagreements now and then. Brothers and sisters, husbands and wives, grandparents and grandchildren all have moments when they just do not get along. These times are frustrating, but they usually do not last long. That is because families are rooted in love. We must remember that we are united by a very special bond at all times.

A good way to illustrate the bond of family unity is to make a folded paper family. From a piece of paper, cut a long strip that is five inches wide. Fold it back and forth like an accordion every two inches. There must be as many folds as there are members of your family (plus two, for good measure). If the paper strip is not long enough for this many folds, extend it by taping another strip to it.

*fig. 1*

Once it is all folded, draw halves of two figures, as shown in *fig. 1*.

Cut out the shapes, being careful not to cut the folds. When you are finished, unfold the paper to see your family – standing united and holding hands. Draw faces and clothes on everyone and send the happy family to your grandparent as a reminder of the ties that bind your family together.

**Materials Needed**
paper, scissors, crayons, colored pencils or markers

**Time Required**
30 minutes

**In The End**
Grandparent will receive a paper portrait of her family holding hands

## OTHER IDEAS

~

Instead of coloring the figures in a realistic way, write words across their joined hands that represent your family ties. For example, "love," "respect," "friendship," "religion," "laughter."

# MY FAMILY TREE

**Materials Needed**
paper & pen, colored pencils, crayons or markers

**Time Required**
1 hour

**In The End**
Child will create a family tree to demonstrate his grandparent's role in beginning a wonderful family

## OTHER IDEAS

~

Have your child write down a list of names he would like to name his own children some-day. Send a copy of the list to the grandparent and save the original, for future reference!

All families are different, but they all have one thing in common. A family is made of people who love each other. Your family may contain sisters, brothers, mothers, fathers, aunts and uncles. They are all small parts of the whole. You might say they are like branches on a tree.

Help your child create a picture of your family tree to send to his grandparent. Start at the bottom of a piece of paper and have him draw two faces. These are his grandparents, and they are at the trunk of the tree. Write their names beneath the faces. Draw a branch coming up from the trunk of the tree for each child that they had. Have your child draw a face for each of them and write their names below them.

Next, have him draw a face next to each of those children who is now married, and label it with the name of the husband or wife. Draw a branch coming up from each of the husbands and wives for each child that they had. One of those children is yours! Have him draw faces and write names for each of the children. By now, he should have a drawing of what looks like a tree. Draw some leaves around all of the faces, and let your child color the family tree with crayons, colored pencils or markers.

Send it to your child's grandparents, and thank them for being at the trunk of the tree. It is from them that the whole family tree branched and grew, and they should be very proud of that.

Our Family History

# TERRIFIC TOTEM POLES

Some North American Indians used to carve totem poles, wooden posts carved and painted with a series of symbols that represented their family's ancestry. The symbols, or totems, were images of animals, plants or imaginative monsters created by the artists. Proud in their totems, family members would post the poles in front of their dwellings and warriors would carry smaller versions with them.

Creating a symbolic totem pole for your family is a fun and easy activity. Cut a few six-inch-long strips of different colored construction paper. The strips can vary in width, generally ranging from one to two inches. You will probably need six to eight of them.

Use an empty paper towel roll as a totem pole. Start at the top of it and wrap one strip around it, securing it with tape or glue. Continue with the remaining strips, each under the next and overlapping slightly until the totem pole is full and you have created different color "totems" along its entire length.

Use markers and your imagination to turn each totem into a creature, real or fictitious, that represents a part of your family. For example, if your father pilots a plane, make an eagle. If your grandmother tells a lot of jokes, make a laughing hyena. Be creative, and have fun. Glue construction paper shapes like wings, dorsal fins, tails and beaks to the pole to add dimension and interest.

Send the finished totem pole to your grandparent to proudly display in demonstration of his family heritage.

**Materials Needed**
paper towel roll, construction paper, tape or glue, markers

**Time Required**
1 hour

**In The End**
Grandparent will see a visual display of his family heritage as created by his grandchild

## OTHER IDEAS

~

Enhance the totem pole with texture by gluing feathers, sand, birdseed, cotton and other things to the totems.

# WHAT'S IN A NAME?

**Materials Needed**
research materials or Internet access, family members' knowledge, pen & paper

**Time Required**
an hour or so

**In The End**
Grandparent and grandchild will learn the significance of their family name

# OTHER IDEAS

~

Let your child create a badge by cutting a 3" circle out of a piece of poster board and taping a safety pin on the back of it. On the front, have him write, "My name is _____. It means _____!" He can make a matching badge for his grandparent, too!

Long ago, people did not have as many names as we do today. They were referred to by one given name and many people had the same name.

When family names, called surnames, were added to distinguish between families, they were arrived upon by different means. Families in some cultures selected a beautiful word from a well-known poem to serve as their surname. In some places, the surname reflected the name of a child's father, like Robertson, Davidson or Williamson. In some, the name was based on the occupation of its owner, like Miller, Baker or Carpenter.

Encourage your child to learn more about your family name and the surname of his grandparent, if it is different from his. This information may be easily learned from an older family member, or it may be more difficult to come by.

There are books in the library that may be helpful in tracking down the origin of your family's name. If you have access to the Internet, let your child see what he can find on the Web. He may be able to find a genealogy Web site or a historical analysis of his name.

Your child should compile all of the information that he learns and make a copy of it for his grandparent. Learning the origin of his name will help your child gain a better understanding of the ancestors whose lives molded his family history. By sharing this knowledge, your child may teach his grandparent something about his family that he did not previously know.

# THIS IS YOUR LIFE

Materials
Needed
photos, access
to color copier,
paper, stapler,
glue, pen

Time Required
2 hours

In The End
Both child and
grandparent
will have a
picture book
about the life of
the grandparent

No doubt, your child has books about almost every subject imaginable. It is important for him to learn as much as he can about every subject so he can be a well-educated person. But does he own a story about a very important subject . . . his grandparent? Probably not. You can fix that!

Sort through your old photos with your child and round up a selection of shots of his grandparent throughout her life. You may not have any of her when she was a baby, or a child or any that show her doing things she loves or posing with people who mean a lot to her. You may have to ask her to send you copies of those as well as some school pictures, birthday party pictures, and wedding pictures. Make two color copies of each of the photos.

Create two blank books by stapling stacks of paper together. Have your child trim the photos and glue them to the pages of the books, creating two copies of a photo book that documents the life of his grandparent. After the photos are in place, help your child go through the book and write a description of each photo. Include the names of everyone in the picture, and any interesting stories surrounding it.

Send one copy of the book to your child's grandparent and let your child keep the other. They will then both own a copy of the biography of a very special person!

## OTHER IDEAS

~

Present this book as a birthday gift to the grandparent.

~

Incorporate information about grand-mother and grandfather and present it as a very special 50th wedding anniversary gift.

# NEWS & VIEWS

**M**ost towns, no matter how small, have their own newspaper. It is circulated among the residents to spread the word about worldwide and local news, sports and weather. There are sometimes special sections featuring home and food, weddings and births, entertainment and business.

Help your child create a paper for your family news. The paper can be one page or many pages, color or black and white. It can be handwritten and drawn or done on the computer. The only necessity is that it be informative. Think of a catchy title incorporating your family name (for example, The Baxter Banner, The Thompson Times, The Daily Dawson).

Then instruct your child to write short articles about your family news. Encourage other family members to contribute. Perhaps your sister wants to write the sports section so she can focus on her swim meet. Maybe Dad wants to write about his business trip in the travel section and Mom is excited about sharing a favorite recipe in the food section. Feature your grandparent as a special columnist, and have him mail you his article to be included in the newspaper.

Once the articles are written, format them in sections with columns, using a real newspaper as a guide. Include pictures that you and your family have drawn or scan photographs into the computer and incorporate them into the sections.

Create a new newspaper every few months, or whenever you have enough news to fill an issue.

# FAMILY PRIDE

**Materials Needed**
pen & paper,
camcorder &
videotape

**Time Required**
1 hour

**In The End**
Grandparent
will receive a
tape of original
family cheers

There are a lot of ways to show enthusiasm and pride. Cheerleaders show pride in their team by writing cheers. Students show school pride by wearing their school colors and singing their school song. States show their pride by creating mottos or slogans.

Family pride is shown in much more important ways. It is demonstrated by its members standing up for each other and for what they know to be right. You see family pride in the way parents raise their children, and children respect their parents. These things are far more significant than a cheer or a song.

But not many families have an official cheer, song or motto. Having your child compose those things is a fun and thought-provoking way for her to verbalize those things that make her proud of her family.

Help your child think of some school cheers and songs as well as a state or business motto. Then, allow her to write her own family song, cheer and motto. When she is finished, get out a tape recorder or camcorder and tape her singing the song, shouting the cheer or reading the motto.

Label the tape "Family Pride" and send it to your child's grandparent, who will swell with pride when watching it.

## OTHER IDEAS

~

Make a family banner out of felt. Paint the family motto on it, or cut out felt letters to spell it out.

~

Decorate a T-shirt with the family motto or words to the family song or cheer.

# THE OLDEN DAYS

**Materials Needed**
pen & paper, video- or audiotape

**Time Required**
1 hour

**In The End**
Grandparent will be interviewed by child to glean knowledge of his life

Most of us have heard stories of our grandparents "walking ten miles to school barefoot in the snow, uphill both ways," and other similar tales. There is a lot to be learned from the past.

To find out about his grandparent's life long ago, have your child conduct an interview. A fun way to do a long distance interview is to have the interviewer (your child) write the questions and send them to the person being interviewed, (his grandparent). The grandparent can then tape himself answering the questions. When complete, that tape will be fun for your child to listen to again and again.

Instruct your child to be thoughtful in choosing the questions and to cover every interesting aspect of life. For example,

## OTHER IDEAS

~

If the grandparent has a camcorder, have him videotape his interview for a more visual finished result.

• What year were you born? • What was a school day like? • What did you do for fun? • Who was your favorite movie star? • Did you have a favorite doll or stuffed animal? • What was your first job? • Did you play a role in any wars? • Tell me about your wedding. • How did you decide what to name your children?

Send the list of questions with a blank tape and instructions for your child's grandparent to tape his answers and mail them back. He will be flattered that his grandchild has an interest in his past, and will create a precious keepsake with his taped response.

# GRAND DOSSIER

· · · · · · · · · · · · · · · · · ·

**D**uring wartime, governments put together a dossier (pronounced "doe-see-ay") on those people they suspected of being spies or double agents. A dossier is a collection of documents and papers about a certain person or subject, often kept in a file. A dossier can contain information on any subject and is helpful in organizing that information.

Your child can use his grandparent as the subject of a dossier. Label a manila filing folder with the words "Grandparent Dossier." Let your child keep it in a desk drawer where it will be easily accessible for updating. In the folder, have him place loose photos and letters he has received from his grandparent.

From now on, use the folder to store all correspondence and information pertaining to his grandparent. Place birthday and other holiday cards, postcards and pictures in the file. Collect momentos, such as napkins from restaurants or programs from plays attended together. If your child learns something new about his grandparent, such as what his favorite book is, have him write that information on an index card and file it in the dossier.

The file will expand through the years and grow fat with information and correspondence that will hold many memories for both your child and his grandparent. One day in the future, they may enjoy looking through the file together and reminiscing.

**Materials Needed**
manila folder

**Time Required**
few minutes throughout the years

**In The End**
Grandchild will create a collection of correspondence and memories from his grandparent to share some time in the future

## OTHER IDEAS

~

Because grandparents tend to spoil their grandchildren, start a list of gifts given to your child from his grandparent. Be sure to note the date it was given and the occasion for the gift. It will be fun to look back on long after the gift has been given.

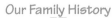

# FOREFATHER'S FROCKS

**Materials Needed**
dress up clothes, camera & film

**Time Required**
1 hour

**In The End**
Grandparent will be flattered to see himself imitated by his grandchild

## OTHER IDEAS

~

**Find props to be held in the photos to further develop each character. For example, if the grandfather is a chef, have your child hold a large whisk or frying pan in the photo where he is dressed like his grandfather.**

Is there a business in the family that members for generations have worked for, or have your parent, grandparents and great grandparents each taken a different career path? Whichever is the case, it is fun to try to picture all of your ancestors dressed for their jobs in the recent or very distant past.

Have your child write down the occupations of his grandparents and ancestors before them as far back as possible. Then, instruct him to research what kind of clothing was worn by people in those occupations. Have him gather clothes and accessories from around the house to simulate the work clothes of his grandparents and other forefathers (and mothers!).

In addition to occupation, it may be interesting to dress up in traditional ethnic clothing of family members who sported Polish, Italian, Greek, African or other traditional garb.

Let him dress up as each ancestor and pose for a photograph in each "costume." You can "label" each photo by writing the name and occupation of each person with a thick marker on a piece of paper. Have your child hold up the appropriate name in each photo.

Send copies of the pictures to your child's grandparent. He may want to frame the one that depicts his grandchild dressed as himself and bring it to work for his co-workers to see.

Grampa Davis

# UNIQUELY ME

# GRAND OLD FLAG

## OTHER IDEAS

Your child can create a flag for her grandparent using colors and symbols that she thinks best represent her grandparent.

In 1776, Betsy Ross made the first flag of the United States. George Washington is said to have designed it and the elements on it had a special significance. Each star and a stripe represented a state in the union – thirteen stars and stripes in all. As the country grew, more stars were added.

All countries have flags with elements that symbolize something important to them. Each state in the United States has its own flag, as does each branch of the armed services. Flags are symbols of pride and should be meaningful in their content and color.

Have your child create a flag for herself. Let her use an old pillowcase or large piece of felt for the flag itself. She can leave it rectangular or cut it into a different shape.

The flag will be an emblem of her, and therefore should feature her favorite colors and have items pictured on it that represent her. Encourage her to choose items that demonstrate her talents, beliefs and hobbies. The items can be cut out of felt or scraps of fabric and applied to the flag with glue. Details can be added with T-shirt paint.

When finished, the flag can hang in her room or on her door as a proud symbol of all that she stands for. Take a picture of your child holding her flag. Have her write an explanation of the elements that are on the flag and enclose the explanation in an envelope with the picture when you send it to her grandparent.

# HELPING HANDS

· · · · · · · · · · · · · · · · · · · ·

E ach person is blessed with a certain talent. Sometimes it is easy to see that talent in ourselves, but often it seems hidden and must be hunted for. Whatever our personal skill may be, it will flourish and grow when we put it to good use by sharing it with others.

Challenge your child and his grandparent to share their skills, talents and time by doing some volunteer work. Let each one determine exactly what kind of work is appropriate for himself.

For example, if your child is a budding musician, he can play the piano once a week at a local rest home. A nature lover can pick up trash at the park and an aspiring doctor can volunteer at the local hospital in any capacity that is needed.

By talking about their volunteer decisions and work, your child and his grandparent will motivate each other and share a special pride. By getting involved in a cause other than their own personal lives, they will each be helping to make the world a better place.

**Materials Needed**
time only

**Time Required**
depends on activity

**In The End**
Grandparent and child will volunteer to help others

## OTHER IDEAS

●

Suggest that your child search the newspaper for stories of people helping others. They are few and far between, but when found, they will inspire your child to continue with his good deeds. When he is finished reading it, have him send the article to his grandparent.

# MY FAVORITE THINGS

**Materials Needed**
pen & paper

**Time Required**
15 minutes

**In The End**
Child and grandparent will learn each other's favorite things

E ven when your child was a little baby, there were certain things that she really liked and others that she didn't. Through the years, the lists of "likes" and "dislikes" has grown and changed. You have been there all along and know her favorites as well as those things she despises.

Help her make a list of favorites and least favorites to share with her grandparent who hasn't been around on a daily basis and may not know that information.

On a sheet of lined paper, make a list of categories down the left side. It will be the first column in the chart. Sample categories to put on the list may include:

## OTHER IDEAS

●

Have your child add a humorous category at the bottom that says, "Favorite Grandparent - YOU!"

| food | animal | book |
| dessert | day of week | holiday |
| fruit | song | team |
| school subject | sport | vegetables |
| teacher | cartoon | television show |
| color | movie star | season |

Write "favorite" and "least favorite" across the top of the paper. As your child writes her favorite and least favorite of each category beneath its appropriate heading, she will be creating the second and third columns of the chart.

When the chart is finished send it to your child's grandparent and instruct him to create his own list and send it to his grandchild. It will be interesting to see what they have in common.

|  | FAVORITE | LEAST FAVORITE |
| --- | --- | --- |
| FOOD | | |
| COLOR | | |
| ANIMAL | | |
| SPORT | | |
| VEGGIE | | |
| SEASON | | |
| TEAM | | |
| SHOW | | |

# PRIZED POSSESSIONS

Remember that stuffed animal or doll that your child's grandparent gave him when he was a baby? It has likely become a faithful friend who sleeps, plays, eats and "talks" with your child. Its fur or hair may have been "loved" off and it has probably been put through the washing machine on more than one occasion.

We may never fully understand why that particular doll or animal was chosen to be "the one." Your child is the only person who may be able to put that into words. It is a good idea to have him do that now, before he gets too old to see the beauty of his "friend."

Give your child a blank thank you card and instruct him to write a pretend note to that prized possession. Tell him to let the doll or animal know why he loves it so much and thank it for all it does for him every day. Have him draw a picture of himself with his special friend to enclose in the note.

Tuck the note away in a safe place to look back on in future years, but not before making a photocopy of it to send to your child's grandparent who will enjoy learning about the prized possession of his grandchild.

Next, have your child write a thank you note from the animal's point of view. The card should be sent to the grandparent, thanking her for giving the animal to the child and listing some of the memories they have made together.

**Materials Needed**
pen & paper, crayons

**Time Required**
30 minutes

**In The End**
Child will thank grandparent for a favorite stuffed animal

## OTHER IDEAS

Have your child write about some of his other prized possessions — a favorite T-shirt, pair of shoes, necklace or ball cap, for example.

Do you still have your old teddy bear or doll packed away somewhere? If so, get it out for your child to see. Who knows, it may become one of his favorites, too!

# WHEN I GROW UP

Materials
Needed
pen & paper

Time Required
15 minutes

In The End
Child shares
thoughts of her
future with her
Grandparent

Children begin thinking about their lives as adults even when they are very young. Dreams of being a super-hero or fairy princess usually change to more realistic aspirations, such as being a veterinarian or teacher. Let's face it, some of us are still trying to decide what we want to be "when we grow up."

These visions of the future are important for our children, and are early forms of goals and dreams that push them to grow, learn and achieve. It is interesting to look back at our own childhood and compare how we pictured our adult life versus how it actually turned out.

Take the time to record your child's dreams of the future so that you can all look at them in later years and compare them to reality. Have your child write a description of how her "grown up" self will be. Issues to consider are:

## OTHER IDEAS

Have your child list things she will definitely NOT do or be in the future. It will be interesting to see if that holds true.

Who will I marry?     What kind of car will I drive?

Where will I live?     What type of home will I live in?

What will my job be?     What kind of pet will I have?

What will I look like?     What will my children be like?

Make a copy of the description and put the original in an envelope. Tuck it away in a safe place and save it for a day in the future when you and your "grown up" child will have a great time looking at it. Send the copy to your child's grandparent so that she can see the aspirations of her grandchild and know what she can look forward to in the future.

# MY BEST FRIEND

You probably see your child's best friend on a fairly regular basis. Between sleep-overs and study sessions, ball games and shopping trips, they are probably together so much that you feel like a parent to the friend as well as your own child.

Unfortunately, your child's grandparent may not get to see the duo in action very much at all. Because a child's best friend is such a significant part of his life, have your child do an activity to let his grandparent get to know his friend a little bit better.

Have your child and his friend interview each other, taking turns asking questions and writing or recording the answers. Challenge them to think of questions that reveal information about their friendship, such as, "Do you remember when we first met?" "What was the funniest thing that ever happened to us?" or "Why do you think we are such good friends?"

Next, have them each draw a portrait of the other. They can

sit across from each other at a table, each with a piece of paper and a pencil, looking at each other and drawing what they see. Encourage them to color the pictures as realistically as possible.

Make copies of the interviews and pictures and send one set of copies to your child's grandparent who will learn a lot about one of his grandchild's most important relationships. Be sure to give your child and his friend copies of their work for their own reminiscing and entertainment.

**Materials Needed**
pen & paper or tape recorder, colored pencils, crayons or markers

**Time Required**
1 hour

**In The End**
Grandparent will learn about his grandchild's best friend

## OTHER IDEAS

Take the kids to a store that has a photo booth and let them have their picture taken together. Send a copy of the photo strip to your child's grandparent.

# FINGERPRINT FUN

# OTHER IDEAS

Let your child spell out his grandparent's name using a series of fingerprints to create the letters.

Have your child create a finger paint picture for his grandparent. Using finger paints or any non-toxic, washable paint, he can paint a picture using his fingers instead of paintbrushes.

Fingerprints can be used as a form of identification because no two people share the same one. Your child's fingerprint is completely unique. Because everything that makes your child unique is of interest to his grandparent, have your child create a picture for his grandparent made primarily of fingerprints.

Use an ink pad or create one by coloring on a small piece of wax paper with a marker. While the ink is still wet, stick your child's finger in it, then press the finger, ink side down, onto a piece of paper to make a fingerprint. You can use multiple colors of markers for a more colorful picture.

After the paper is full of fingerprints, let your child use markers to transform each print into a little work of art. He can make animals and people, insects and flowers. The prints can be made into trains, planes, cars or houses. Let his imagination run wild!

When the picture is complete, write your child's name on it and stick it in the mail to his grandparent. That fingerprint picture will be a very welcome gift and will serve as a reminder of the person who owns the little fingers that created it.

# ALL ABOUT ME

Your child is most likely familiar with autobiographies. He has probably read several for school assignments and may have even done a book report on them. If your child has not yet read an autobiography, go to the library together and find one about someone your child is interested in. Have him read it to gain an understanding of the concept of an autobiography.

Of course, this is in preparation for an activity. You guessed it . . . have your child write his own autobiography!

It does not need to be lengthy, but the autobiography your child writes about himself should be informative. Have him discuss the major events of his life in chronological order. His own birth, learning to walk and talk, birth of a sibling, and moving to a new school are examples of events he might want to mention.

Have him also mention minor events along the way that he finds memorable or that influenced his life in some way. These might include a family vacation, victory at a spelling bee or learning a new sport.

The text of the book can be written on loose-leaf paper and put into a three-ring binder. Photos can be inserted on special photo pages or on the pages of the autobiography that mention the events that they portray. Send the finished book to your child's grandparent. It will probably become his favorite book!

**Materials Needed**
loose-leaf paper, pen, three-ring binder

**Time Required**
2 hours

**In The End**
Grandparent will receive an autobiographical account of his grandchild's life

## OTHER IDEAS

On your child's birthday each year, have him update his autobiography by writing a new page that covers the events of the past year. Send it to his grandparent for insertion into the binder.

# LIFE QUILT

• • • • • • • • • • •

**Materials Needed**
felt, scissors, dowel rod, glue, string, ribbon

**Time Required**
1 1/2 hours

**In The End**
Child will create a quilt with a very personal pattern

Quilts do a great job of keeping us warm on cold nights. They have become much more than blankets, though. Quilts are practically an art form of their own. From geometric to realistic, quilts boast designs and colors that can be breathtaking in their beauty. So beautiful are some, in fact, that they are hung on walls to be displayed rather than tossed on beds to provide warmth.

This no-sew activity is a way to create a "quilt" wall hanging that uses its panels to tell a very important story — the life of your child. Cut a piece of felt, (or other thick fabric you may have), to a 14" x 12" rectangle. Fold the top two inches of the fabric over a 14" long dowel rod and fasten it with a line of glue, as shown here *(fig. A)*.

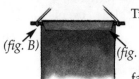

*(fig. B)*        *(fig. A)*

Tie each end of a long piece of yarn to the ends of the dowel. This will be the hanger for the quilt *(fig. B)*. You are now left with a 12" x 12" square of fabric. Divide it into nine 4" squares by gluing 12" long pieces of thin ribbon onto the fabric in a grid-like formation *(fig. C)*.

You have created a "quilt" with 9 panels. Your child can cut shapes out of old scraps of fabric or colored felt to glue into

each square. The shapes should represent something about your child and can be in chronological order of her life. For example, a pacifier, teddy bear and tricycle followed by a soccer ball, school book and ballet shoe.

Send the finished quilt to your child's grandparent. It will be a meaningful piece of art and a lovely decorative wall hanging.

*(fig. C)*

# CAMEO APPEARANCE

Materials
Needed
bright lamp,
white paper,
tape, pencil, black
construction
paper, scissors,
glue

Time Required
30 minutes

In The End
Grandparent
will receive a
silhouette of
his grandchild

The art of capturing images has certainly come a long way from the old tintypes of the past. With all of our technological advances, the art of photography has grown and flourished. Unfortunately, one beautiful way of displaying a likeness of a person has been virtually lost: the silhouette. The single-color images of people's profiles that used to hang on walls and be inserted into jewelry are not seen very much today.

Silhouettes are so easy to make that there is no reason not to revive this lost art to capture the image of your child's distinct profile. Simply sit your child down sideways in front of a wall. Set a bright lamp or other bright light next to him with the light shining on the side of his face and casting a shadow of his profile onto the wall. This works best in a dark room.

Tape a piece of white paper to the wall, positioning it so the shadow is right in the middle. Using a pencil, lightly trace around the shadow to create a profile on the paper. After that is done, remove the paper from the wall and hold a piece of black construction paper behind the sketch of the profile.

Using a sharp pair of scissors, your child can carefully cut along the pencil line you drew, cutting through the white

## OTHER IDEAS

The white cutout of the silhouette can be saved and used as a template for creating another silhouette for your own use or to insert into your child's scrapbook.

and black paper simultaneously. When finished, there will be a black silhouette of your child that will look great glued on a white background and displayed in a frame at his grandparent's house.

# NEW NAMES

● ● ● ● ● ● ● ● ● ● ● ● ● ●

Materials
Needed
pen & paper
Time Required
45 minutes
In The End
Child will think
of a new, mean-
ingful name
for his
grandparent

There are few things that all people have in common. One of those things is a name. We all have one. Some of us like ours, some of us don't. Some of us go by a nickname, others prefer their given name. Our parents likely chose our name before they even knew us.

Encourage your child to learn the meaning of his name and his grandparent's name. Have your child write down the meanings of the two names and give some thought as to whether they adequately describe their owners. There are books in the library full of names and their origins and meanings.

## OTHER IDEAS

●

Child and grandparent can both assign new names to all of their family members and then compare what they came up with.

Some Native Americans gave descriptive names to their children once the children were old enough to display certain characteristics or talents. A name like "Running Horse" may be given to a child who runs fast, and one like "Little Petal" given to a petite little girl who loves flowers. Native Americans receive several names throughout their lifetime.

Have your child think of a new name for his grandparent and himself. They can be real names that have specific meanings or made-up names. The only criteria is that they be fitting and meaningful for each personality. Once the names are selected, let your child illustrate each one. The illustration can be realistic or symbolic.

Send your child's grandparent his "new name" with its illustration. He will be interested to see how he is perceived in the eyes of his grandchild.

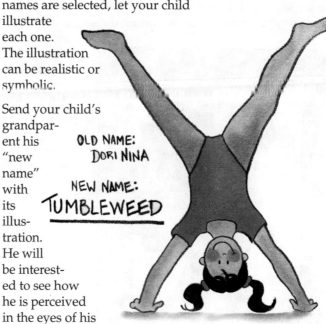

OLD NAME:
DORI NINA

NEW NAME:
TUMBLEWEED

# TIME CAPSULE

●●●●●●●●●●●●●●●●

**D**esigned to aid scientists and scholars of the distant future to understand our contemporary culture, a time capsule is a sealed container preserving articles and records. Although our own personal lives may not be of vital interest to future scientists, it is fun to put together a time capsule to look back on ourselves someday.

This is an activity that your child and his grandparent can work on together whether or not they live in the same town. Instruct them each to gather items that represent the world around them. Magazine advertisements, grocery store circulars, candy bar wrappers and automobile brochures are good items to include. Other ideas would be a record of a hit song, catalog pages of latest styles, a list of popular words and expressions (and their definitions), or the movie listings from the newspaper (with the date remaining on the top of the page).

**Materials Needed**
box, packing tape, various paraphernalia

**Time Required**
1 hour

**In The End**
Child will create a time capsule to be enjoyed with his grandparent some time in the future

Pack the items in a box and seal it with packing tape. Write "TIME CAPSULE" on the box and note the date it was packed. Let your child and his grandparent think of a date in the future that they want to open the box. Perhaps on the child's 30th birthday, New Year's Eve of a certain year, or maybe exactly 20 years from the day the capsule was sealed. Write "Do Not Open Until _____ (the date you have chosen)" on the box and put it in the attic, garage or other safe storage place.

Leave it there until that date in the future when it can be unsealed and enjoyed. You will all be quite entertained on that day and will be very glad that you took the time to make your own time capsule.

## OTHER IDEAS

●

Include personal items in the box such as photos, programs from school performances, birthday cards and letters to and from one another.

# WISH LIST

· · · · · · · · · · ·

**Materials Needed**
magazines, scissors, glue, construction paper

**Time Required**
1 hour

**In The End**
Grandparent will learn what sort of material things his grandchild longs for

# OTHER IDEAS

•

**Try collages with other themes:**

• Things I can be when I grow up

• Grandparent's favorite things

• Things that are my favorite color

• Some of my favorite foods

Young children already have desires for material things. Material belongings cannot provide true happiness. Though belongings are just "things" and are not important in the grand scheme of things, it is fun for children to imagine owning everything their heart desires.

Help your child make a collage to send to his grandparent. It can be used to illustrate his favorite things and those things he wishes he had. Gather up some old magazines and a pair of scissors. Have your child browse the pages of the magazines and cut out pictures of things that he would like to have.

After a nice assortment of images has been cut out, glue them all to a piece of construction paper. Let the images overlap each other and cover the whole page, or leave space around each one for a descriptive caption. When complete, the collage will be a good representation of things that are wished for by your child. His grandparent will enjoy looking at the collage and talking to his grandchild about all of the things represented therein.

# AUTHOR, AUTHOR

Because your child has read so many books, (or has had so many read to her), she has probably experienced almost every kind of story there is. She has read happy stories and sad ones, exciting and dangerous adventures as well as tender stories about friends and love. With her imagination, she can think of a story just as good as the ones she has read, so have her write and illustrate a book to send to her grandparent.

First, create a blank book by stapling several pieces of paper together with a line of staples down one side. Then challenge her to think of a story. Explain to her about the parts of a story (characters, setting, and plot), and the necessity to develop each. Once she has figured out the whole story in her head, have her write it down in the pages of the book, starting on the third page. Save the first page as the cover and the second page for the dedication page. Write only a sentence or two of the story on the top or bottom of each page of the book, leaving room for illustrations.

Next, have her work with pencils, crayons or markers to create colorful illustrations on each page of the story. The goal is to show the reader what the characters, places and events look like.

Have your child write a dedication note to her grandparent on the blank second page of the book telling him that the book was made especially for him. Package the book in a large envelope and send it to your child's grandparent. Surely, the story will bring more excitement and happiness to her grandparent than your child's own books bring to her.

Materials
Needed
paper, stapler,
pencils, crayons,
markers

Time Required
1 1/2 hours

In The End
Child will create
an original
storybook to be
enjoyed by her
grandparent

## OTHER IDEAS

●

After reading
your child's
book, write a
stunning book
review on the
back cover!

# MY FAVORITE FAN

**Materials Needed**
sports memorabilia, pen

**Time Required**
15 minutes

**In The End**
Grandparent will receive a valuable autograph

**M**ost sports figures have fans who follow their careers and cheer for them through the years. It is the fans who often inspire the athletes to go the extra mile and strive to achieve excellence. Without fans, most sporting events would not be much fun at all.

Famous athletes thank their fans by signing memorabilia such as baseball cards, programs and ball caps. Their autographs are often valuable.

If your child is involved in sports, his family members are likely big fans. His grandparent may not get to see him play as often as he would like, but is undoubtedly the biggest fan of all.

## OTHER IDEAS

If your child's grandparent cannot attend his games, videotape one and send the tape in the mail.

Let your child pretend that he is a famous sports star. Whether he plays soccer or baseball, football or basketball, he can find some "valuable collectible" to autograph and send to his grandparent. A baseball cap or sweat sock would be perfect, as would a knee pad or football jersey. He can even create his own sports collectors card by posing for a photograph in his uniform. Once developed, the "card" can be autographed.

Whatever item he chooses to send, your child will be certain to please his "Number One Fan"—his grandparent.

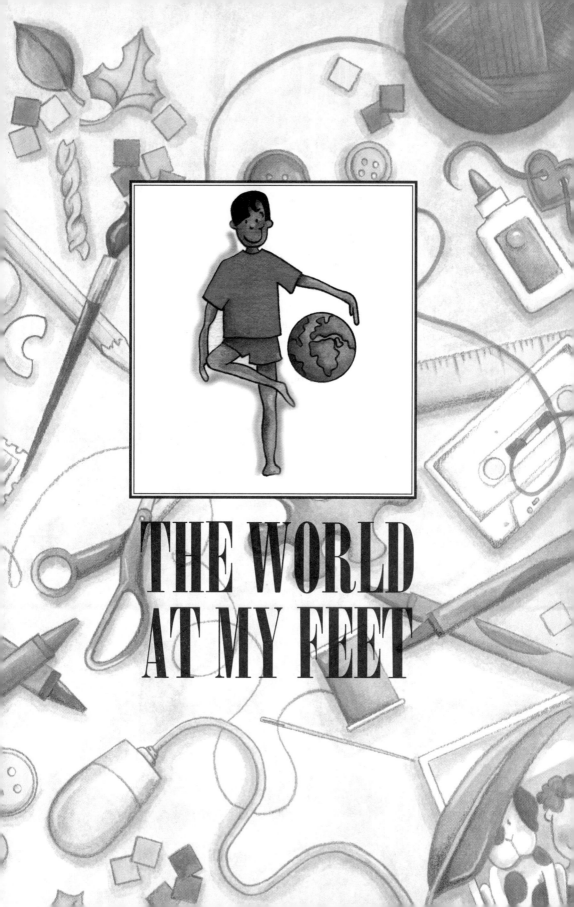

# THE WORLD
# AT MY FEET

# ANIMALS ON PARADE

**Materials Needed**
zoo, notepad or spiral notebook, pen

**Time Required**
1 1/2 hours

**In The End**
Child will share a day at the zoo with his grandparent

## OTHER IDEAS

Your child can use an encyclopedia or the Internet to learn more about specific animals.

A trip to the zoo is guaranteed to be full of interesting sights, sounds and smells. The next time you go, share the experience with your child's grandparent by having your child create a sheet of Zoo Notes.

Let your child carry a notepad or spiral notebook and pen as you walk through the zoo, and encourage her to jot down interesting facts and observations along the way. Be patient, and allow for frequent stops, because the zoo is full of interesting things.

Think of some fun honors to bestow upon the animals that you see, such as: loudest, slimiest, funniest or stinkiest animal. Remind your child to document all of the winners in her notebook.

Carefully compare and contrast the different habitats of the animals and make note of those differences. Challenge your child to look for things that other visitors to the zoo may not notice, such as which food was left over by the monkey or where each animal sleeps. Ask zoo officials questions to learn information about feeding schedules, daily routines and mothering skills of the animals.

Encourage your child to make quick sketches of unusual markings on certain animals or of features that are unusual, like a funny "hairdo" or unusually large nose on a monkey.

After your visit, make a photocopy of the Zoo Notes to send to your child's grandparent. He will almost feel as though he was there with you.

# SOWING SEEDS

• • • • • • • • • • • • • • • •

There are few things as fascinating as a seed. It starts as a tiny object, and with the proper amounts of water, nutrients and sunlight, grows into a plant that can be taller than a grown man.

Let your child and her grandparent share in the gratifying task of growing a seed. This spring, buy two packets of sunflower seeds. Give one to your child and send the other to her grandparent.

Have your child create a growth journal so that she and her grandparent can monitor the growth of their flowers. The "journal" can be very simple, consisting of a single column of dates listed down the left side of several pieces of paper. The first date should be the "plant date," the day the seeds are to be planted. Select a plant date that is about a week after you plan to mail the seeds, preferably a Saturday. Each following date in the journal should be one week after the previous date.

On the "plant date," both gardeners should follow the instructions on the packet and put their seeds in the ground. Using a ruler to measure the plant each week, they should record its height and any other notes that may be appropriate, such as development of leaves or blooming of flowers, on the corresponding date in the journal.

When the flowers are full-grown, each gardener should have a photograph taken of themselves standing next to one of their flowers to send, along with a copy of their journal, to the other gardener. At the end of this activity, they will have nurtured seeds as well as their own relationship and have had the pleasure of watching both grow and flourish.

## Materials Needed
paper, pen, seeds, camera & film

## Time Required
couple of minutes as plant grows

## In The End
Grandparent and child learn how to grow something from seed

# OTHER IDEAS

Those gardeners who do not have a place to plant seeds outside can plant beans, tomatoes or peppers in pots on a balcony or in a window.

# ELECTION DAY

- - - - - - - - - - - - - - -

**Materials Needed**
newspapers, pen & paper

**Time Required**
an hour or so to read the newspapers, then a few minutes to fill out the ballot

**In The End**
Child will gain an awareness of political issues and compare his opinions with those of his grandparent

## OTHER IDEAS

Get involved in your child's school and organize a smaller version of the polls on election day. Photocopy ballots for the kids and hold a mock election, announcing the winners over the loudspeaker at the end of the day.

Every few years, we have the opportunity to go to the polls and let our vote count toward the selection of elected officials. Because kids under the age of 18 do not have this privilege, they are often oblivious to the entire thing. Here is a way to involve them in election day and encourage them to start thinking about the leadership of the country in which they live.

Before election day, have your child read the newspapers to keep up with the important issues and to compare the opinions of the candidates with his own beliefs and values. Call the campaign headquarters of specific candidates and request information on their platforms. Contact the Republican and Democratic Party offices to request informative literature on their positions on important issues.

Let your child follow the pre-election news and determine who he would vote for if he were old enough to do so. Most newspapers run lists of the candidates the day before or the day of important elections. Give your child that list and a pen and instruct him to "vote" for his choice in candidates by circling their names on the list.

Discuss his choices after his voting is done. He will likely have very good reasons for the decisions he made. Send a copy of his "ballot" to his grandparent, who will be interested to see if his grandchild votes the same way he does. The two can debate the issues and learn more about each other.

# NIFTY NICKNAMES

Materials
Needed
pen & paper
Time Required
45 minutes
In The End
Child will think
of new names
for animals

One of the most thought-provoking tales in the Bible is the very quickly mentioned event of Adam naming the animals. It is hard to imagine a world full of creatures so newly created that they did not even have names. Even more difficult to imagine is the job of coming up with names for all of them.

Pretend that your child is playing the role of Adam. Make a list of animals, or better yet, find a book of animals with photographs of many different species. Give your child a pen and a pad of paper, and her assignment: "Think of a new name for all of these animals." Then let her imagination run wild.

The names can be serious or funny. They can be based on physical characteristics or habitat, color, size or personality. The names can be short or ten syllables long. There are no rules.

When the activity is complete, send the list to your child's grandparent. He will probably like the newly created names better than the conventional ones.

## OTHER IDEAS

Since your child will be giving the animals new names, let her also suggest some "design changes." Maybe, if it were up to her, the elephant's nose wouldn't be so long, or the dog would walk upright on his two hind legs. See what kind of ideas she comes up with.

HORNBLAT

# CONSTELLATION EXPLORATION

●●●●●●●●●●●●●●●●●●

**Materials Needed**
star chart

**Time Required**
few minutes
each night

**In The End**
Child and grand-
parent will learn
about the stars
and moon

## OTHER IDEAS

Let your child
create an
indoor "starry
sky." Take a
brown paper
grocery bag
and place it on
a carpet. With
a nail, have
your child
punch holes
through the
bag in the for-
mation of the
constellations.
Insert a small
lamp or bright
flashlight into
the bag and
see the light
shine through
the bag and
cast lighted
images of the
constellations
on the walls
and ceiling in a
dark room.

If your child and his grandparent live in different towns, there are few things that they will see on a daily basis that the other can see as well. The stars can be seen by both of them on any given night, and can help them feel connected to each other though they may be miles apart.

A study of the stars can be interesting for both your child and his grandparent, giving them a mutual learning experience. Constellations are groups of stars that form patterns in the sky that can be interpreted as pictures of mythological characters, animals and inanimate objects. Learning to identify the constellations is a great starting point for the beginning astronomy enthusiast.

Search your library or the Internet for a star chart, which is like a map of the locations of the more visible star formations. Make a copy for your child and one for his grandparent. Let your child and his grandparent discuss a schedule for learning how to spot each of the major constellations.

As they walk outside each night to learn their mutual lesson, they can feel connected by the knowledge that the other is looking at the same sky and the same stars. In addition to the layout of the stars, they can also study the phases of the moon and observe its changes.

# SHARING AND CARING

● ● ● ● ● ● ● ● ● ● ● ● ● ● ● ● ● ● ● ● ● ● ● ● ●

**Materials Needed**
extra money

**Time Required**
a few minutes throughout the year

**In The End**
Grandparent and child will donate money to a good cause

**M**any children today have more toys than they could ever play with and more books than they could ever read. We pride ourselves on being able to give our children material things. It is important to stress to our children, though, that happiness does not come from material things. Family, health and love are some of the things we should cherish and that bring us exceeding joy. Sharing and helping other people is another way we can receive happiness.

It is important for our children to understand there are children in the world without toys and books. Families without enough money. Your child can learn how to achieve true happiness by sharing some of her own good fortune with those less fortunate, and this lesson can be learned in a fun way with this activity with her grandparent.

Challenge your child and her grandparent to talk about different charitable organizations and to select one that is meaningful to them. Have them pledge to give to the charity 10% of their "extra" money for one year. This money can come in the form of birthday money, allowance or gifts for the child. For the grandparent, it may be bonuses, gifts or "eating out" money.

Have them each collect their money in a special box or envelope throughout the year and then send it to their charity at the end of the year. Knowing that they have helped someone in need should bring great joy to both of them.

## OTHER IDEAS

Have your child and her grandparent volunteer their time in addition to their money. Visitors at nursing homes, for example, are always welcome and bring great joy to the residents there.

# ON THE MONEY

●●●●●●●●●●●●●●●●●●

**Materials Needed**
paper, pencil, money
(to study, not spend!)

**Time Required**
2 hours

**In The End**
Child will learn an appreciation and knowledge of money

## OTHER IDEAS

Help your child make a list of people or places that he thinks should be pictured on money.

Your child's grandparent has probably sent him money on occasion. Did he look at it very well? Does he know that on every coin or piece of paper money made in America, there is a picture of a man on one side and a picture of a building, animal or something else on the back?

Your child can show his grandparents that he truly appreciated any money that they or anyone else has ever given him and has studied each and every piece of it.

Show your child one of each kind of coin and paper money that you have. Get two pieces of paper and arrange the money on one of them. Trace around each piece of money with a pencil. Then write below it what it is, (for example, quarter, penny, one dollar bill, ten dollar bill). Repeat this process on the other piece of paper.

Label one piece of paper "Front of Money," and label the other piece "Back of Money." On the "Front" paper, have your child draw the picture of each of the men on the front of each of the pieces of money. He will find their names written on the paper money and can write that beneath each drawing. You will have to help identify the person on each coin so your child can label them, too. Next, have him draw the scenes on the backs of all of the money.

Then, challenge him to do some research to learn something about every scene or man on every piece of money. He can use the Internet, encyclopedia or dictionary to help him and should record his findings on another piece of paper. When he is done, send all that he has done to his grandparents. They will share your pride in all the hard work your child did to learn about money.

*The World At My Feet*

# ANIMAL MIX-UP

• • • • • • • • • • • • • • • • • •

**Materials Needed**
index cards,
scissors,
pencil, crayons,
colored pencils
or markers

**Time Required**
1 hour for child,
20 minutes for
grandparent

**In The End**
Grandparent
and child create
and name an
assortment of
funny animals

**A**nimals are designed certain ways for a reason. Giraffes have long necks to reach their food in the trees, and it is obvious why fish have gills and scales. The animals are most likely happy with their current configuration, but it is fun to think about what an elephant would look like with a long neck or how a cat would function with a trunk.

Your child can easily make a set of mix-and-match animals and have a lot of fun arranging and rearranging them. Give your child a stack of index cards and instruct him to draw an animal on each one. The animals should be drawn in profile, and they should all face the same direction.

Next, cut each card into three pieces, one containing the head, one the middle section, and one the rear end. Your child can mix up the body parts and put them back together in any way he wants. For example, a bear head, bird body and snake tail.

Have your child tape some of these funny created animals together and send them to his grandparent with instructions to assign each one a name. For example, the combination mentioned above could be called a "Serpent-Tailed Flying Grizzly." Once named, the animal cards can be sent back to your child, who will surely be entertained by their funny names.

# OTHER IDEAS

Use animal pictures cut out of a magazine instead of drawing them by hand.

Cut out different human faces from magazines, cut them into four pieces, one to include the left eye, one for the right eye, one to include the nose, and one for the mouth. Mix and match these facial "puzzle pieces" to create funny faces.

# TRAVEL BROCHURE

Sometimes, grandparents cannot travel to see you as often as you would like. You must remind your child that regardless of where he lives, her grandparent loves her very much and misses her when they are not together. Help them remember past visits and look forward to future ones by making a travel brochure to send to the grandparent about where you live.

To create a travel brochure of her own, your child will need a clean piece of paper and a lot of imagination. Fold the paper into thirds to create three sections on the front and three sections on the back of the paper.

Encourage your child to think of six nice things about where she lives. These can be about her house, pet, family or backyard. Or they can be things to do or places to visit in her hometown. Instruct your child to create a picture of one of the things in each section of the brochure. She can draw the pictures or cut out and glue some pictures found in magazines or elsewhere. Then have her write a brief description of each thing in its own section. Trying to make everything sound wonderful, to convince the "traveller" to come to the places she is promoting in her brochure, or prompting him to remember times spent there in the past.

When she is finished, send the brochure to the grandparent. Let the grandparent know that your child is very much looking forward to his next visit and can't wait for them to actually see and do everything described in the brochure.

## OTHER IDEAS

Ask your child's grandparent to send real travel brochures from where he lives for your child to look at and learn from.

# RAY OF SUNSHINE

● ● ● ● ● ● ● ● ● ● ● ● ● ● ● ● ● ● ● ●

**Materials Needed**
paper & pencil
**Time Required**
20 minutes
**In The End**
Child will fill grandparent's day with sunshine

While your child is enjoying a beautiful, sunny day, it is possible that his grandparent is experiencing a rain storm. Weather is an interesting thing, and it can be fun for your child to track the weather in his grandparent's home town.

Have your child prepare a special reminder of a sunny day to share with his grandparent the next time her weather is gloomy.

Send your child outside on a sunny day with a pad of paper and a pencil. Instruct him to lay the pad on the ground on top of interesting shadows that he sees and to trace around them, thereby transferring their shape to the paper.

Shadows especially fun to trace are those of trees with intricate branches and twigs, flowers and plants in the garden. Sometimes, a butterfly will remain perched on a flower or a bird will pause and sing long enough for your child to trace their shadow.

Then, watch the national weather report, and when you see a rainy system headed for your child's grandparent's part of the country, stick the shadow pictures in the mail. When they arrive, the grandparent will be treated to thoughts of his grandchild and visions of a bright, sunny day.

## OTHER IDEAS

Suggest that your child trace around the shadow of his own hand or that of a friend making animal-shaped shadows on the paper.

# AMERICA THE BEAUTIFUL

**Materials Needed**
pencil & paper

**Time Required**
1 hour

**In The End**
Grandparent and child share thoughts about America

## OTHER IDEAS

Have your child create a new song, motto and flag for the state in which he lives and the state in which his grandparent lives.

One nation under God, America is truly beautiful and proud. Our country boasts every natural wonder from oceans and mountains to forests and plains. Songs have been written about the land and its people. Even the states that comprise it have their own state mottos and emblems.

Pretend for a minute that this fine country had no national anthem. No flag. No symbol.

Encourage your child to think about that and to compose his own original national anthem for the United States. He and his grandparent can brainstorm and make a list of their thoughts and feelings about the country in which they live. Then, they can arrange the thoughts into a new national anthem. It can be set to the tune of an existing song, or it can just be written like a poem.

Have them also designate a national animal, devise a motto, and design a new flag for our country. All of this should be done with great thought as to what our country represents and strives to convey to the world.

Make copies of everything so that both creators can retain a copy of all that they created. It will be interesting for each of them to see the way the other sees the country in which he lives.

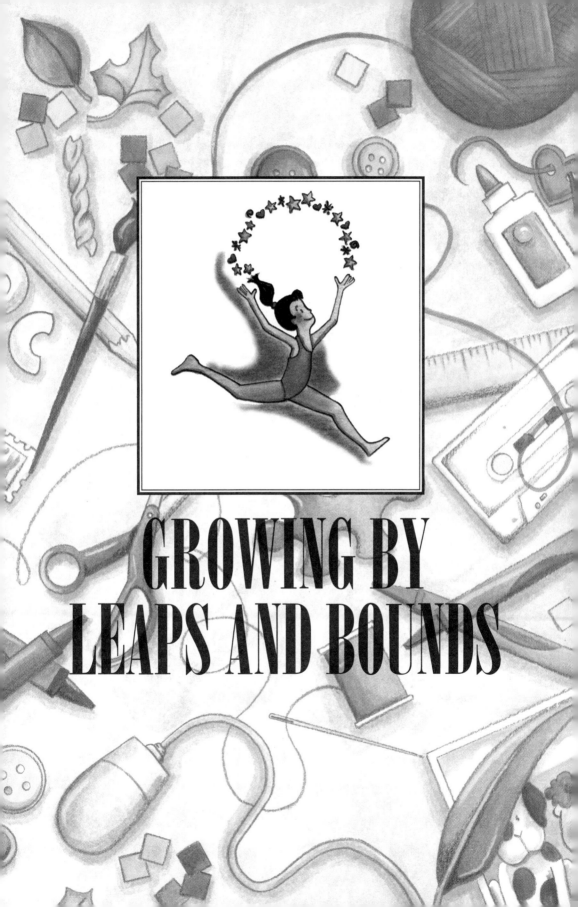

# GROWING BY
# LEAPS AND BOUNDS

# PLASTER CAST

● ● ● ● ● ● ● ● ● ● ● ● ● ● ● ●

## Materials Needed
pie plate, vaseline, plaster of Paris, water

## Time Required
1 hour

## In The End
Child makes a handprint cast for his grandparent

## OTHER IDEAS

▲

Let your child paint the finished plaster cast or color around it with markers. Spray it with polyurethane glaze. Allow it to dry.

▲

Your child can create a plaster cast of his foot in addition to that of his hand.

There are many people who lived long ago who will never be forgotten because their image has been captured in a statue. Although most fine artists carve statues out of marble, your child can make a fine work of art out of plaster and capture her hand print in time.

Grease a pie tin with vaseline, spreading it all around with a piece of paper towel. Mix up a small batch of plaster of Paris according to the directions on the container. Pour the liquid mixture into the pie tin, filling it up to about 1/4" from the top.

Allow it to partially harden. It will set rather quickly, so you will have to keep a close eye on it. When it is the consistency of thick mud, rub vaseline all over your child's hand and gently press his hand (fingers spread) into the plaster right in the center of the pie tin. Push it down a bit, but not far enough to cover the fingers. Lift the hand back out, and the hand should have left an impression in the plaster. (NOTE: If the plaster is too runny and the print fills back in, simply wait a little bit longer and do it again.)

Once the plaster is completely dry, place your hand on top of the pie tin and slowly invert it to release the plaster cast of your child's hand. Use a marker to neatly write your child's name and the date above or below the hand impression or on the back of the cast, if desired.

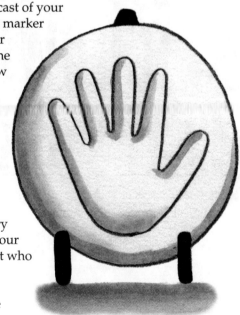

Carefully wrap the cast in tissue and pack it in a box with packing peanuts, as it is very fragile. Send it to your child's grandparent who can use it as a paperweight or display it in a plate easel.

# LITTLE ME

● ● ● ● ● ● ● ● ● ● ● ●

Y ou may have a bag somewhere in your house full of unmatched socks, torn pantyhose and scraps of fabric from old shirts and pants. Let your child put these things to good use by creating a small model of herself for her grandparent to have.

Find a pair of pantyhose with at least one foot that is in good condition. Let your child cut off one leg of the pantyhose and bunch it up into a compact ball. Stuff the ball into the other leg, pushing it all the way down into the foot. Then, tie a string around the base of the ball, forming a head and neck of a little doll.

Stuff some more pantyhose or other balled-up fabric in beneath the tied "neck" to form a body. Tie the bottom of the "body" in a knot and cut off any remaining pantyhose below it. Arms and legs can be made by cutting off the fingers of an old glove, stuffing them with cotton and sewing or gluing them in place on the doll's body.

Once the body is assembled, the fun really begins. Let your child decorate the doll to look just like herself. She can use any kind of supplies she can think of — yarn for hair, beads for eyes, real makeup to add color to the face. She can make her favorite outfit out of felt or scrap fabric you have around the house. The goal is to make the doll look as much like herself as possible.

When finished, send the doll to your child's grandparent. It is not as good as having the real grandchild there, but it will be an entertaining substitute.

**Materials Needed**
socks, pantyhose, scraps of fabric, string, cotton, needle and thread or glue, yarn, beads, etc.

**Time Required**
2 hours

**In The End**
Grandparent will receive a doll that resembles his grandchild

# OTHER IDEAS

▲

Let your child make her doll a pet dog or cat that looks like her real pet.

# FIT AS A FIDDLE

● ● ● ● ● ● ● ● ● ● ● ● ● ● ● ● ●

**Materials Needed**
bodies!

**Time Required**
a few minutes each day

**In The End**
Grandparent and child will grow physically stronger while strengthening their relationship

**T**hese days, there is quite an awareness about health and fitness. All studies point to the fact that an active lifestyle can lead to better health. Exercise is a vital part of that lifestyle.

Any exercise program we try to adhere to is more successful when we have someone to help motivate us – a buddy who either exercises with us or who cares enough to check up on us on a regular basis to ensure that the exercise is being done.

Your child and his grandparent can begin a regimen of exercise and help motivate each other to successfully continue it. Because their bodies are undoubtedly quite different, they should exercise differently. There are some things, though, that will likely benefit them both. Things like stretching, walking, sit-ups and jumping jacks are good for almost everybody.

Have the two discuss what kind of exercises they each plan to do and how often they plan to do them. Then, it is their responsibility to check on one another every once in awhile and request a progress report of how well the other has stuck to his exercise program.

## OTHER IDEAS

▲

The exercisers can send each other little handmade awards for special accomplishments along the way, like when the grandparent first walks a mile or the grandchild does 50 sit-ups.

They should encourage each other to do a little bit more each time. If your child is doing ten jumping jacks three times a week, his grandparent can suggest he do fifteen starting next week. If the grandparent is walking around the block each day, your child can suggest he walk one mailbox further next week. This program will be mutually beneficial and will build stronger bodies and hearts.

# LEND A HAND

● ● ● ● ● ● ● ● ● ● ● ● ● ● ● ●

Your child's hand prints are uniquely his own. Those unique hand prints can be used to create original pictures of animals or other things. It is surprising how many things contain "hand-like" shapes. Your child can probably think of quite a few.

Give your child a large piece of paper and some washable paint. Have him paint the palm of his hand with the paint and then press it down onto the paper to create a hand print. There must be some thought put into the way the prints are arranged on the paper, because the next thing he will do is turn those prints into pictures.

For example, with a marker or paintbrush, two hand prints placed side by side can be transformed into antlers on top of a deer's head. One upside-down hand print can become an octopus, (well, a "pentopus," actually, with five legs). Four or five hand prints placed in a circle with all of the fingers pointing out can be a bright yellow sun full of "finger rays" or a brightly colored flower with lovely "finger petals."

The possibilities are endless! Once the picture is finished and dry, send it to your child's grandparent. He will enjoy seeing the creative ways his grandchild can transform his hand print into real works of art.

**Materials Needed**
paper, washable paints, markers

**Time Required**
1 hour

**In The End**
Child makes hand-print pictures for grandparent

## OTHER IDEAS

▲

Send a special card to your child's grandparent on Thanksgiving featuring your child's hand transformed into a turkey's profile. The thumb becomes the neck and head (just add an eye, beak and gobble), the other fingers are feathers along his back. Draw some legs and feet, and there you have it!

# WHAT'S INSIDE ?

● ● ● ● ● ● ● ● ● ● ● ● ● ● ● ● ●

As your child grows, he starts to understand that his "tummy" is really called a stomach and it aids in the digestion of food that he eats. He learns that his heart is not really shaped like a valentine, and it plays a very important role in his life.

Here is an activity to teach your child a bit about some of the organs in his body and also to keep in touch with his grandparent. Have your child lay down on a large sheet of butcher paper and trace around him with a pencil, making a life-size drawing of his body. Erase the inevitable "slip of the pencil" marks, and then use a marker or crayon to go over the drawing you made.

Using an anatomy book or other reference material, have your child draw his organs in the proper places on the drawing of his body. Be sure he includes the brain, lungs, heart, kidneys, liver, intestines and stomach. Other organs, bones and muscles can be included, if desired.

## OTHER IDEAS

▲

Cut out life-size clothing to place over the drawing and tape the clothing on one side to create flaps that open up to reveal the organs inside. Let your child color the clothes to match his favorite outfit.

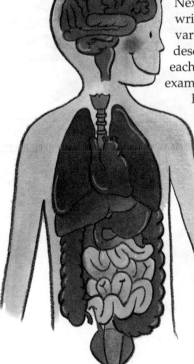

Next, have him take a regular writing pen and make notes on various parts of the body, describing each part and what each has been up to lately. For example, "This is my brain. It has had a hard time learning geometry." Or: "My stomach digested five pieces of pepperoni pizza last night!"

When finished, roll or fold up the drawing and send it to your child's grandparent. It may be too large to put on the refrigerator with the other artwork, but it will be exciting to receive a life-size educational drawing of such a knowledgeable grandchild.

# GROWTH CHART

Growing may be the thing that your child does best. He certainly does it every day with or without your permission. In fact, you could not stop it from happening, even if you wanted to!

We monitor the growth of babies so well and note their progress in baby books for future reference. There is really no reason to stop that interest in your child's growth when he ceases to be a baby. Because you see your child every day, you may not realize how quickly he is growing, so this activity will benefit you, too.

Have your child step on a scale every few months (maybe the first day of each season, so you will remember when four months have gone by), and record his weight. Record his height, too, and send the information to your child's grandparent, written on the back of a recent photo of your child.

The grandparent can keep all of the photos in chronological order in an envelope, box or photo album. Through the years, she will have collected an informative and pictorial progress report of the growth of her grandchild. It will be almost like being there to watch him grow up.

**Materials Needed**
paper, pen, photographs, scale, ruler

**Time Required**
a couple of minutes every few months

**In The End**
Grandparent will be able to "watch" her grandchild grow

## OTHER IDEAS

Have your child illustrate a border all around the edge of a piece of paper labeled "Growth Chart" and send it to his grandparent. The grandparent can use this sheet to record each reported growth.

Trace your child's hand or foot, sending the tracing to the grandparent with the growth report.

# CLIP, CLIP, CLIP

## Materials Needed
camera, film, (OPTIONAL: hair barrette, scissors, plastic zipper lock bag)

## Time Required
45 minutes

## In The End
Grandparent will enjoy seeing grandchild before and after haircut

## OTHER IDEAS

▲

Have your child draw a picture of himself both before and after the haircut. Remind him to draw facial expressions that accurately portray how he felt throughout the haircut experience.

Those beautiful silky locks of hair. Curly or straight, black or blonde, each little strand is precious. Eventually, of course, measures must be taken to tame that growing "do." Thus, the haircut.

Whether the haircut takes place in the beauty parlor, barber shop or in the kitchen, document the occasion on film. Take pictures of your child from the front, side and back before the hair is cut. Take pictures of your child while the hair is being cut. Finally, take more pictures of the final result.

Be sure to save some locks of hair that are cut off. Place some of the precious locks in a plastic zipper lock bag. For little girls, if there are curls involved, gather some individual ones in hair barrettes before cutting. Clip off the whole curl, barrette and all. The barrette will do its job of holding that curl for years to come. Store locks of hair in zipper lock plastic bags, or enclose some in a picture frame, keepsake box or a locket.

After the pictures have been developed, write the date on the backs of them and send copies of them, along with a lock of hair, to the child's grandparent.

BEFORE     AFTER

# BIRTHDAY REPORT

• • • • • • • • • • • • • • • • • • •

You always hear about how quickly time flies, but never fully understand what that means until you become a parent. No sooner do you welcome your new baby into the world, than you are celebrating his first birthday and the years just fly by after that. Every birthday is a special day and brings memories to parents and grandparents of that wonderful day when their child or grandchild was born.

If your child's grandparent cannot be with him on his birthday, create a birthday report to send to him so he can know what the special day was like.

Have your child jot down a description of how he celebrated and a list of who was there to share the big day. Take lots of photos and note your child's favorite gift. Write down what kind of cake was eaten and what was the most memorable moment of the day. Have your child tell you whether he feels older and explain her goals for the upcoming year. Record his answers.

Send all of this party information to your child's grandparent, thereby including him in the celebration of the special day.

## Materials Needed
paper, pen, camera & film

## Time Required
30 minutes

## In The End
Grandparent will be included in child's birthday celebration

# OTHER IDEAS

▲

Take a special picture of your child on her birthday holding a sign that says, "Wish You Were Here." Include it in the birthday mailing to her grandparent.

▲

Have your child make a collage using scraps of wrapping paper to send to his grandparent.

# CLEAN CLOSETS

**Materials Needed**
old clothes

**Time Required**
1 hour

**In The End**
Grandparent and child learn to help others

## OTHER IDEAS

Encourage your child and his grandparent to look into the possibility of doing some volunteer work at the Goodwill or Salvation Army. They would likely be grateful for help in sorting items that they receive.

Considering the steady growth of your child and her wild growth spurts, it is very difficult to keep her in clothes that actually fit.

No sooner do you purchase a pair of pants, than they are too short. She may wear a dress for only a month before it rises too high above the knee to be acceptable.

Kids really do grow like weeds, and clothes that no longer fit pile up in their closets. Every once in awhile, go through your child's closet with your child. Make a stack of those items of clothing that are no longer wearable.

Have your child call her grandparent and challenge him to go through his own closet and make a stack of items that he no longer wears.

Bag up the clothes, tell the grandparent to bag up his clothes, and designate a day on which you will all head to your local Goodwill or Salvation Army thrift store.

Donating old clothes is good for everyone involved. It helps you to clean out your closets. It enables others who may be of limited means to purchase clothing at very low prices. Perhaps most important, it develops a sense of community and togetherness, respect for property and love for others. By sharing this experience with his grandparent, it becomes even more meaningful for your child.

# DRESSING UP

● ● ● ● ● ● ● ● ● ● ● ● ●

**D**ressing up like someone else is fun, no matter how old you are. Children especially enjoy it and go about it with much enthusiasm.

Allow your child to look through all of the closets in the house and find an outfit that he thinks his grandparent would wear. Let him dress up like his grandparent. Help him accessorize and fix his hair to resemble his grandparent as closely as possible. This can be quite hilarious, especially if your child and the grandparent are of the opposite sex.

Take some pictures of him posing doing things that his grandparent likes to do and send the pictures to his grandparent. Your child will have a blast assuming the role of his grandparent, and his grandparent will get a real kick out of seeing himself imitated.

**Materials Needed**
dress-up clothes, camera, film

**Time Required**
30 minutes

**In The End**
Grandparent will see himself through the eyes of his grandchild

## OTHER IDEAS

▲

Videotape your child playing the role of his grandparent. Ask him questions, and instruct him to answer them as he thinks his grandparent would.

# THE LATE SHOW

**Materials Needed**
television, telephone, popcorn

**Time Required**
2 hours

**In The End**
Grandparent and child will watch a movie "together"

## OTHER IDEAS

The next day, have your child and his grandparent each write a movie review of the movie they saw and assign it either a "thumbs up" or "thumbs down." They can mail each other the reviews and see if they are in agreement.

Growing older usually means "staying up late." This rite of passage is one of the most anticipated of all. For years, your child has gone to bed at an early hour, imagining the parties that his parents must certainly have once he falls asleep. As he ages, the bedtime is usually pushed back, and he gets to stay up later and later.

This privilege is special and exciting. Of course, it will not take long for your child to learn that staying up late is really not such a big deal. But it does have its advantages.

Let your child share a late night with his grandparent. Check the television listings and find a movie or documentary that looks like it would be of interest to both your child and his grandparent. Send a pack of microwave popcorn to the grandparent with a note of the day, time and television station of the program he will be watching "with" his grandchild.

On the planned night, each participant can pop his popcorn and watch the movie in his respective home. They can call each other before, during and after the movie to chat and share their opinions. When all is said and done, they will have shared a very special evening together. Two "adults" staying up late.

# SMELLY SNEAKERS

**Materials Needed**
old sneakers, nylons, potpourri, decorative items, glue

**Time Required**
1 hour

**In The End**
Child will create something useful from old shoes

Sneakers, like other clothes of growing children, are grown out of quickly. For some reason, kids often become sentimentally attached to their sneakers and hate to give them up even after they can no longer squeeze their feet into them.

Here is a way to turn those old sneakers into useful items for your child's grandparent. When your child grows out of a particularly favorite pair of sneakers, transform them into wonderfully "smelly sneakers." Smelly in a *good* way!

Purchase a bag of potpourri and scoop a couple of cups of it into each foot of an old pair of nylon knee highs. Tie the "bags" of potpourri closed with some string and insert one into each sneaker.

Next, give your child an assortment of items with which to decorate his sneakers. Fabric paint, sequins, lace and beads are great items to use.

Once decorated and filled with potpourri, the shoes are transformed into sachets that your child's grandparent can hang by their laces in her closet. The sneakers will fill the closet with a lovely scent and fill your child's grandparent with memories of her thoughtful grandchild.

## OTHER IDEAS

Use old socks instead of shoes. Fill them with potpourri and tie them at the top. Whether you use sneakers or socks, the irony of the "smell" still exists.

# ALL GROWN UP

● ● ● ● ● ● ● ● ● ● ● ● ● ● ● ● ●

**Materials Needed**
paper, pencil

**Time Required**
30 minutes

**In The End**
Grandparent will see how his grandchild imagines herself as an adult

Children think a lot about what it will be like to be grown up. What will they be? Where will they live? How will they look? That last question may be at least vaguely hinted at by the way their parents look, but nobody will know for sure until it happens.

Your child has likely drawn a lot of pictures of herself through the years. Her drawings probably depict a child playing or learning. Challenge her to draw a picture of herself the way she imagines herself looking when she is an adult.

This activity will require some thought. Remind her to consider clothing and hair styles as well as facial features. Her drawing can be of the face only, or include the entire body to allow the viewer to see an entire outfit.

When finished, send the picture to your child's grandparent and let him see if there is any similarity between his future grandchild and her current self.

## OTHER IDEAS

▲

Tell your child to draw her future self doing something, whether it be working, playing or standing outside her future home.

# PRINT WORTH A MINT

**R**emember when you used to get into trouble for leaving hand prints on the walls or footprints down the hall? Children have a way of leaving their mark wherever they go.

Though it may seem frustrating now to have to wipe little prints off of your walls and constantly scrub the floors, the time is not distant when the child who owns those hands and feet will be old enough to know better. So, you had better savor every dirty moment.

Let your child send some hand and footprints to his grandparent for his walls. Spread some colorful paint all over a piece of paper. Press child's hands and bare feet, one at a time, into the paint, then stamp them onto a clean piece of paper.

After the paint is dry, label the feet and hands pictures with the name and age of the child. These little prints will be received well by the grandparent, and don't require any cleaning!

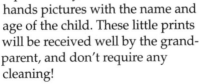

If your child would like, let him compose a poem to accompany the prints, such as:

*Little hands, little hands leave prints upon your walls.*

*Little feet, little feet running down the halls.*

*Here's a little token of my feet and hands so small*

*To help you to remember them when I'm grown big and tall.*

---

**Materials Needed**
non-toxic paint, paper

**Time Required**
30 minutes

**In The End**
Grandparent's walls will be adorned with hand and footprints

# OTHER IDEAS

▲

Do hand, finger and footprints on card stock to create postcards

▲

Decorate the border of a piece of paper with finger prints to create stationery

# TOOTHY GRIN

## Materials Needed
black, red & blue pens, paper

## Time Required
a few minutes for each tooth

## In The End
Grandparent will stay abreast of child's dentistry

S tarting at around age six, your child will begin to lose his 20 baby teeth and begin growing a full set of 32 adult teeth.

Because his grandparent will likely not be there for each exciting loss of a tooth, your child can keep him informed of his "tooth status" and learn more about his own teeth.

Have him check out a book from the library about teeth and, using a black pen, draw a chart of his mouth based on what he learns. Basically, the chart should look something like *fig. 1*.

Photocopy the chart several times. Each time your child loses a tooth or two, have him color the respective tooth on a copy of the chart and note the date it fell out. He can mail the chart to his grandparent and include a note about other news in his life.

upper teeth
incisors

canine

premolars

molars

premolars

canine

incisors
lower teeth

*fig. 1*

Continuing this process throughout the loss of all of the baby teeth will guarantee two things. First, your child will be knowledgeable about the names of all of his teeth, and second, his grandparent will receive a lot of mail! It will be a "win-win" situation.

# CALENDAR EVENTS

# SUNCATCHER

• • • • • • • • • • • • • •

## Materials Needed
evergreen sprigs, berries, pine cones, etc., pie tin, water, string

## Time Required
1 hour

## In The End
Grandparent will see how his grandchild is spending the cold winter days

## OTHER IDEAS

✦

In case of a temporary warm spell in the weather, simply pop the suncatcher into the freezer to preserve it until the freez-ing tempera-tures return.

✦

Make a birdfeed-er to hang on a branch near the suncatcher. Simply cover a large pine cone with peanut butter and roll it in birdseed. Hang it by a string.

C old winter weather can keep us indoors and make us long for the warm days of spring when the world is blooming with new life. If we are not careful, though, we may miss the natural beauty of winter. If the cold air where you live stays below freezing in the winter, making a wintery suncatcher is a wonderful way to capture some beautiful winter greenery as well as to add some decoration to a near-by tree.

First, have your child gather some sprigs of evergreen, bright red berries and tiny pine cones, acorn shells or sweet gum

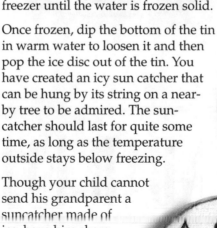

**JANUARY**

balls. Arrange the items in a pie tin and fill the tin with water. Fold a 10" long string in half and drop the ends of it into the water-filled tin, leaving the rest of it out of the water. Place the tin in the freezer until the water is frozen solid.

Once frozen, dip the bottom of the tin in warm water to loosen it and then pop the ice disc out of the tin. You have created an icy sun catcher that can be hung by its string on a near-by tree to be admired. The sun-catcher should last for quite some time, as long as the temperature outside stays below freezing.

Though your child cannot send his grandparent a suncatcher made of ice, have him share the idea with her in case she wants to make one of her own. Besides, a photograph of your child stand-ing outside beside his icy creation will brighten her day as much as the actual suncatcher would.

# NEW YEAR'S RESOLUTIONS

As each year comes to an end, we all tend to make lists of things we intend to do differently in the year to come. These resolutions sometimes change our lives for the better, but are more often forgotten after a month or so. Your child and his grandparent can share their New Year's Resolutions with each other and try to help each other keep them throughout the year ahead.

## JANUARY

On January 1, have each one of them write down their resolutions for the new year as well as a plan for bringing each of them to fruition. They can each photocopy their list and send a copy to the other.

Then, after the year has gotten under way, they can keep each other in check about their respective resolutions, talking about them every month or so to monitor progress.

## RESOLUTIONS
1. Make better grades.
2. Be more helpful around the house.
3. Make some new friends.
4. Don't fight as much with brother.
5. Learn Spanish.
6. Take horseback riding lessons.
7. Go to school dance.
8. Eat more vegetables.
9. Get black belt in karate.
10. Spend more time with grandparents.

By joining together on this mission of resolutions, your child and his grandparent will serve as a conscience for each other and may wind up actually keeping their New Year's resolutions, a feat few of us can accomplish.

**Materials Needed**
pen and paper

**Time Required**
20 minutes

**In The End**
Grandparent and grandchild will help each other keep their New Year's resolutions

## OTHER IDEAS

Have your child and his grandparent make a promise to each other about the upcoming year having to do with their relationship. For example, they may promise to talk more often or send each other more letters.

# "LOVE"LY LETTERS

**Materials Needed**
pen, paper, envelopes & stamps

**T**his "back and forth" Valentine's Day activity will require a lot of stamps, but will be worth the investment. Your child and her grandparent will send a piece of paper back and forth to each other, adding one line to it each time.

**Time Required**
a few minutes each turn

On a lined piece of paper, write "I Love You Because..." across the top. Then, down the left side, write the letters of the alphabet, one on each line, like this:

**In The End**
Grandparent and child will exchange an alphabet of compliments

A _____

B _____

C _____

D _____

*(continue until the alphabet is complete)*

## OTHER IDEAS

✦

If the back and forth idea does not appeal to you, let your child fill out the entire alphabet on her own with words about her grandparent. Then, instruct her grandparent to do the same for her.

✦

Let your child use a computer to e-mail the list back and forth instead of using traditional mail to send it.

Let your child take the first turn to fill in the line by the letter "A" with a characteristic that she loves about her grandparent. For example, "You are so Adventurous." Then, she can send it to her grandparent who will fill in the "B" line with something like, "You are so Bright."

This activity will continue to run its course until the entire alphabet has been used. Whoever winds up with the finished piece may photocopy it and send a copy to the other.

Grandchild and grandparent will both look forward to receiving their "alphabet love" sheet in the mail and will have great fun thinking of flattering adjectives to describe the other.

# FOLDED FLAKES

● ● ● ● ● ● ● ● ● ● ● ● ● ● ● ● ● ●

N o two snowflakes are alike. Each is unique. The same holds true for people. Each one is special. Have your child make some snowflakes to symbolize the beauty of winter as well as the miracle of her own individuality.

## FEBRUARY

○ ○ ○ ○ ○ ○ ○

Using thin white paper, have your child cut some squares and some circles of paper. Next, he should fold each shape in half, then in half again. He can then begin to cut small shapes out of the edges of the folded paper, cutting through all of the layers of paper with each cut.

**Materials Needed**
white paper, scissors

**Time Required**
30 minutes

**In The End**
Grandparent will receive handmade snowflakes

When unfolded, the paper is transformed into the one and only snowflake of its specific design. Let your child make a lot of snowflakes to decorate his room. He can send some of them to his grandparent who will certainly be thrilled to receive an envelope full of unmelted snowflakes in the mail. Encourage him to include a note explaining that just as each snowflake is unique, his grandparent is truly one of a kind and irreplaceable in the eyes of his grandchild.

## OTHER IDEAS

Spread glue over the snowflakes and sprinkle them with silver glitter to make them sparkle and shine like real snowflakes touched by the sun.

# LACE EGG

● ● ● ● ● ● ● ● ● ●

## OTHER IDEAS

◆

**S**ymbols of new life and rebirth, eggs are delicate and precious things. They have become synonymous with the Easter holiday, as it falls in the spring and celebrates new life.

## MARCH

○ ○ ○ ○ ○ ○

A fun way for your child to create a decorative and very beautiful egg is as follows:

Have her dip a very long piece of yarn into white glue and wrap the yarn around and around a small balloon in a very random manner. Continue wrapping until the balloon is almost completely covered.

After the glue dries, pop the balloon with a pin and carefully pull it out of the egg shape that has been created. The egg that remains will look like it is made of delicate lace.

Let your child make several small "lace" eggs and send them to her grandparent to decorate her house in the spring. The eggs are conversation pieces, and she will get to brag about her grandchild to anyone who comments on the fragile-looking little decorative eggs.

# APRIL SHOWERS

**Y**our child has probably heard the expression "April showers bring May flowers." The expression is true in both a literal and figurative way. Not only do the rains of the early spring help flowers to grow, but also "rain" in one's life helps people to grow. Many things that we consider to be bad or unpleasant wind up teaching us valuable lessons or becoming something very good. Teach your child the meaning of this old adage with the following activity.

**APRIL**

Cut three raindrop shapes out of light blue construction paper. Have your child glue three cupcake cups toward the bottom of a large piece of paper. They will be the centers of three flowers. Your child can cut out colorful construction paper petals for the flowers and glue them around the centers. Next, have your child glue one raindrop a few inches above each flower.

Explain the "April Showers" adage and help your child to think of three times in his life when something he did not like later turned out to be a blessing in disguise. Times when something bad turned into something good. Have him write the "bad" things on the raindrops and the "good" things on the flowers to illustrate what grew out of the experience.

When the project is complete, it will be a perfect illustration of the concept of letting a little bit of rain fall into our lives. Without the rain, we would not have the flowers. Sharing this concept with his grandparent will prove mastery of the idea and will surely impress his grandparent.

**Materials Needed**
construction paper, cupcake cups, glue, pen, scissors

**Time Required**
1 hour

**In The End**
Child will learn that even hard times can be learning experiences

## OTHER IDEAS

Have your child call his grandparent and admit to a time when something his grandparent did or said was not understood or liked at the time, but later turned into a "flower."

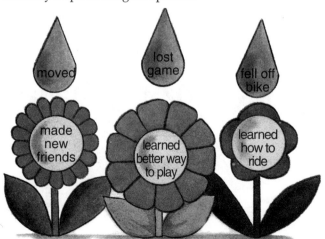

# FLOWER POWER

**MAY**

## Materials Needed
T-shirt, handkerchief or scarf, cutting board, newspaper, leaves and flowers, rock, wax paper

## Time Required
1 1/2 hours

## In The End
Child will decorate an item for his grandparent using leaves and flowers

## OTHER IDEAS

◆

Make a set of cloth napkins for the spring using the rock-tapping technique with petals of spring flowers.

**M**ost plant parts, such as leaves and petals, contain coloring substances that give them their natural beauty. If crushed, that coloring substance can get out and stain whatever it touches. This explains the green grass stains on clothes that have been worn while rolling around playing in the grass. Your child can take advantage of the staining property of leaves and flowers to create a beautiful t-shirt, handkerchief or scarf for his grandparent.

First, have him place a T-shirt, handkerchief or scarf on a cutting board. If using a T-shirt, place a stack of newspaper inside the shirt. If using a scarf or handkerchief, place the stack of newspaper beneath it.

Let your child gather an assortment of leaves and brightly colored flowers. Have him arrange the flowers and leaves beneath the fabric of the item he wishes to decorate, sandwiched between it and the newspaper beneath. He should then lay a piece of wax paper on top of the item and use a large rock to start tapping the cloth in each place where there is a flower or leaf. As he taps, the color will be released by each petal or leaf and be absorbed into the fabric.

When finished, he will have created a shirt, handkerchief or scarf of rare natural beauty. Send it to his grandparent, who will then own a unique item not available in any store. Instruct the grandparent to hand wash the item to keep the colors as vibrant as possible.

WAX PAPER

# IN YOUR HONOR

**G**randparent's Day is a special day set aside to honor those special members of our family who honor us every other day of the year—our grandparents. It is a time for everyone in the family to acknowledge how much the older members of the family have contributed to make the family what it is today.

Let your child do something extra special for his grandparent on Grandparent's Day. Buy a little tree sapling from a plant

## SEPTEMBER

nursery and help your child plant it in honor of his grandparent. First, select a place in your yard that would be a good place for the tree to grow. Follow the nursery's instructions to dig a hole and plant the baby tree.

Take a picture of your child planting the tree. Glue the picture to the outside of a homemade card and let your child write the greeting on the inside. He can explain that he has committed to care for and nurture the little tree and watch it grow, just as he has committed to care for and nurture his relationship with his grandparent. Both will grow and change throughout the years.

Your child can start a tradition of sending a photo of himself next to his "grandparent's tree" ever year on Grandparent's Day. His grandparent will love to see his little tree (and his little grandchild) grow and flourish.

**Materials Needed**
sapling, shovel, camera & film

**Time Required**
45 minutes

**In The End**
Child will plant a tree in his grandparent's honor and help it grow through the years

# OTHER IDEAS

Planting a tree is a nice thing to do to commemorate the birth of a new baby in your family or in loving memory of a loved one who has passed away.

# SPOOKY TREE

· · · · · · · · · · · · · · · · · · ·

**Materials Needed**
paper, drinking straw, black paint, water

**Time Required**
45 minutes

**In The End**
Grandparent will receive a spooky picture and share spooky stories with his grandchild

## OTHER IDEAS

✦

**Draw owls and bats in the tree to enhance the spooky theme.**

✦

**Pop some popcorn and glue the popped kernels to the tree to transform it into a cheerful spring tree in full bloom.**

After the leaves fall off of the trees in Autumn, the trees are left to stand on their own through the long, cold winter. On bright, moonlit nights, the bare trees cast spooky shadows onto the ground.

The shadows are exact replicas of the branches and twigs on each tree, and are quite intricate in their patterns. Your child can make his own spooky tree using just three things.

Have your child add some water to some black paint until it is runny. Stick the end of a plastic straw into the paint and cover the top hole of the straw tightly with your finger. This traps a small amount of paint inside the straw. Move the straw over a piece of paper and release your finger, dropping the paint onto the paper.

**OCTOBER**

Tell your child to point the straw at the watery blob of paint on the paper, holding it very close to, but not touching the paint. Have him blow through the straw and watch the paint "run" from the air. Each time he blows, the ink runs further, branching out into smaller streams of paint along the way. After applying several blobs of paint to the paper and blowing it out to form branches, your child will have created a tree with an intricate branch structure. Send the tree picture to your child's grandparent.

Have your child include a note to his grandparent instructing him to telephone the child when he receives the picture. After discussing the spooky tree, the two can share spooky stories and giggle about how silly the stories really are.

# FRIENDLY GHOSTS

- - - - - - - - - - - - - - - - - - - - - -

C elebrate Halloween by having your child make these little ghosts to hang around his grandparent's house. They are so cute that they haven't got a chance of scaring anyone.

Your child can place a large cotton ball in the center of a white facial tissue and wrap the tissue around the cotton, tying it

## OCTOBER

shut with a piece of thread to create a head and neck. Next, have her create little hands by tying thread around the outer corners of the tissues after folding them over a little bit.

**Materials Needed**
white tissues, cotton balls, thread, black marker

**Time Required**
30 minutes

**In The End**
Child will help grandparent decorate his house for Halloween

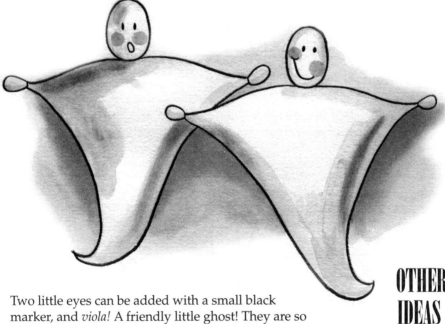

Two little eyes can be added with a small black marker, and *viola!* A friendly little ghost! They are so simple, your child can make a bunch of them. Send some to your child's grandparent and he can hang them here and there to decorate for Halloween.

## OTHER IDEAS

✦

Glue a small ring of silver pipe cleaner onto the head of the "ghosts" to create angels!

# THANKFUL TURKEY

● ● ● ● ● ● ● ● ● ● ● ● ● ● ● ● ● ● ● ● ● ● ●

**Materials Needed**
construction paper, scissors, glue

**Time Required**
1 hour

**In The End**
Child will express her gratitude for the blessings in her life

## OTHER IDEAS

◆

Let those present at your Thanksgiving celebration create a "thankful turkey." Have a feather at each place setting, and allow each person to write on his feather at least one thing for which he is thankful. Assemble the turkey and hang it up for all to see.

**F**all is a time of harvest. It is when all of the hard work in the fields pays off with bountiful vegetables and grains. One of the most meaningful days of the year is observed in the fall – Thanksgiving. The word "thanksgiving" really sums up what

NOVEMBER

we are supposed to do on this wonderful holiday – give thanks for all that we have received. The pilgrims and Indians had a lot to be thankful for at their first Thanksgiving celebration, and so do we.

A good tradition to start for Thanksgiving is to go around the table before the big meal and give everyone an opportunity to tell what he is thankful for. Most importantly, we must remember to be thankful for our family.

Let your child create a "thankful turkey" for his grandparent. Draw a turkey's body on some paper and cut out a lot of colorful feathers to glue onto its back. Before attaching each feather to the turkey, have your child write something she is thankful for on each one.

If the grandparent is able to be with you on Thanksgiving day, your child can deliver the turkey herself. If that is not the case, simply put it in the mail and let the mailman deliver it for her.

It is important to give thanks every day for the blessings in our life, and to never lose sight of how fortunate we are. Upon receiving your child's turkey, her grandparent will be thankful for such a thoughtful grandchild.

# NUTTY ORNAMENTS

• • • • • • • • • • • • • • • • • • • • • • • •

Squirrels stash a supply of nuts sufficient to feed them all winter. They begin to do this well before the air turns cold and winter is upon them. Surely, the squirrels will share some nuts with your child this fall to enable him to create fun-filled nutty ornaments for his grandparent.

## NOVEMBER

Supply your child with several English walnut shells, cracked open and emptied to create two empty halves. Instruct your child to replace the nuts with special little presents for his grandparent. These can be little jingle bells, seashells, beads, marbles or rocks. They can be Bible verses written on little rolled-up pieces of paper or special notes folded up.

Close each little gift between the two halves of each nut, sealing them with a little glue. Seal a loop of string between the halves to use for hanging each nut ornament.

When dry, send the nuts to your child's grandparent. He can hang them from door knobs or window locks, cabinet knobs or his rearview mirror. When he needs a quick pick-me-up, he can crack one open to reveal the special present inside.

## OTHER IDEAS

◆

Let your child turn nut shells into nutty critters. Simply glue jiggly eyes, pipe cleaner legs, antennae and paper wings to nut shells to create adorable little creatures.

you to know that I l... much!

# PUMPKIN TREATS

**Materials Needed**
pumpkin, paring knife, vegetable oil, salt, camera or crayons and paper

**Time Required**
1 1/2 hours

**In The End**
Child will have a carved pumpkin and grandparent will enjoy pumpkin seeds and pictures of the child's pumpkin

## OTHER IDEAS

◆

Allow your child to dress in her Halloween costume and pose beside the pumpkin in the photo or to draw herself in the picture with the pumpkin.

Fall is full of beautiful colors and smells, fruits, vegetables and falling leaves. Halloween is one of the most fun parts of the season, and gives children an opportunity to be very creative. Of course, Halloween would not be complete without pumpkins. Those glorious orange vegetables serve as canvases for decoration as well as sources of delicious food.

Share the holiday experience with your child's grandparent by sending him a tasty snack and picture of his grandchild's pumpkin. After selecting a "perfect" pumpkin, help your child to cut a "lid" out of the top. Let her scoop out all the seeds and "goop" from inside the cavity of the vegetable. A metal spoon with a good sharp edge is the best tool for the job. Separate the seeds from the "goop" and rinse them in water. Allow them to dry on a piece of wax paper.

**OCTOBER**

Once dry, toss the seeds with vegetable oil to coat them and spread them on a baking sheet. Bake at 350° for about an hour, stirring them occasionally so they will brown evenly. Once brown, sprinkle them with salt, allow them to cool, then package some seeds in a plastic zipper bag and send them to your child's grandparent. Carve the pumpkin and take a photograph of it or have your child draw a picture of it to enclose in the envelope with the seeds.

# CHRISTMAS SWIRLS

In all of the hustle and bustle of the Christmas season, it is easy to simply purchase any decorations and ornaments we may want from the stores.

## DECEMBER

We must remember, though, that the most special decorations are those made by children and the most precious memories of the holidays are those involving the crafts and projects in preparation for the big day.

Here's a very easy way to create a festive swirl decoration. Starting on the outside rim of a paper plate, cut a spiral around and around toward the center of the plate, creating a "snake" about one inch thick. Hold onto the end of the "snake" which is in the very center of the plate, and lift it up. The paper will coil down in a lovely spiral shape. Punch a hole in the end of the coil and attach a loop of yarn so the decoration can be easily hung.

Decorate the swirls with glue and glitter. To make small swirls suitable for hanging on the Christmas tree, use small circles of construction paper instead of paper plates. Let your child make several, and send them to his grandparent.

**Materials Needed**
paper plate, scissors, hole punch, yarn, glue, glitter

**Time Required**
25 minutes

**In The End**
Child will create holiday decorations for his grandparent

## OTHER IDEAS

◆

Try creating triangular or square swirls by using shaped paper rather than round plates. Follow the shape of the paper as you cut the spiral to create a unique decoration.

# DANCING SANTA

**Materials Needed**
poster board, scissors, metal brads

**Time Required**
45 minutes

**In The End**
Child and grandparent will be reminded of the spirit of giving around Christmas time

## DECEMBER

Santa Claus is the personification of the spirit of Christmas, a time when Christians remember the greatest gift of all time — the baby Jesus. Christmas is a time of celebration of Jesus' very special birth. At that first "birthday party," the baby was given gifts of gold, frankincense and myrrh. Today, Christians give each other gifts at Christmas and children look to Santa Claus as one of the greatest of gift givers.

Often called Saint Nicholas, Santa's history can be traced back to the patron saint of children with that name. He represents thoughtfulness and generous giving to others, a concept that should be in our hearts through all of the seasons.

Although Jesus is the reason for Christmas, it is fun to think about Santa, who has come to being thought of as a jolly old elf who wears a bright red suit and rides in a sleigh pulled by flying reindeer delivering toys to all the good children of the world.

Here is a fun and simple way for your child to create a "dancing" Santa. Draw and color a picture of Santa on a piece of poster board. Cut the picture out and then cut off its arms and legs. Reattach the arms and legs to Santa's body with metal fasteners, called "brads." Once attached in this way, the arms and legs will be able to move back and forth and make Santa look like he is dancing.

Send the dancing Santa to your child's grandparent to hang on the wall as a happy reminder of the spirit of giving.

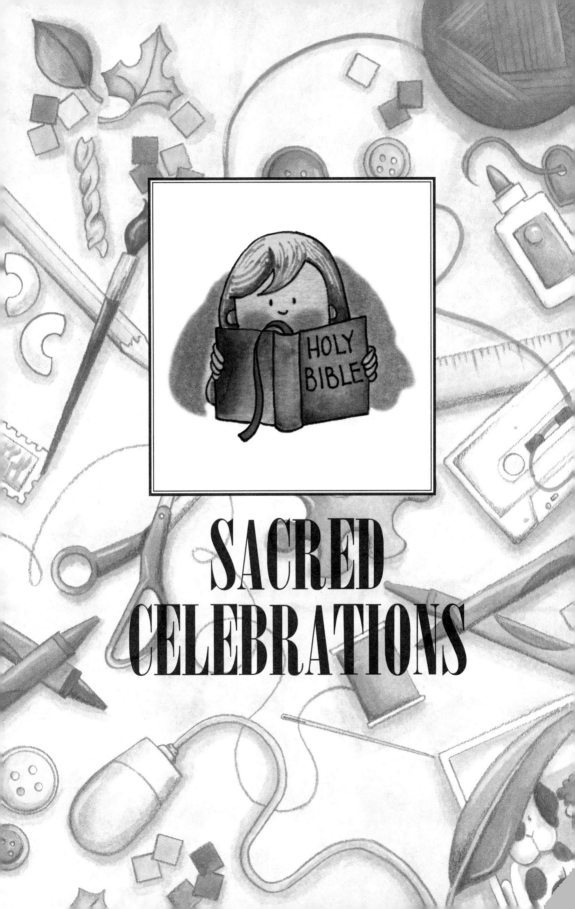

# SACRED CELEBRATIONS

# BOOK OF LIFE

● ● ● ● ● ● ● ● ● ● ● ● ●

**Materials Needed**
time only

**Time Required**
a few minutes

**In The End**
Child will try to mend relationships with grandparent and others

## OTHER IDEAS

◆

Let your child mail a handmade card of apology to those people whose forgiveness she seeks.

The ten days between the Jewish New Year, "Rosh Hashanah," and the Day of Atonement, "Yom Kippur," are referred to as the Days of Awe. During this time, Jewish people believe they are being judged by God.

Each person's name is brought up for review, and names of very good people are entered in the *Book of Life*. During the Days of Awe, a person helps to ensure her name will be included in the *Book of Life* by admitting any bad deeds and trying to make things right in all relationships.

No matter what your religion, this is a good time to remind your child to always do good deeds and to mend relationships that need attention. Talk to your child about things that she did in the past that may have left her feeling sorry or ashamed. Explain to her the importance of taking responsibility for her actions and asking those she has wronged for forgiveness. Encourage her to literally go to those people whom she may have hurt in any way, by word or by deed, and to apologize and ask for forgiveness.

Have her specifically think about whether there is anything she needs to apologize to her grandparent for. If so, she must make a phone call to her grandparent and ask for forgiveness.

We should try to nurture the spirit of doing good and making right of relationships, keeping it alive in our hearts all year long. As the Hebrew expression goes, "Hatimah Tovah!" or "May you be inscribed and sealed in the *Book of Life*."

*Sacred Celebrations*

# DREIDLE DAYS

The Jewish celebration of Hanukkah commemorates the time in Jerusalem long ago of the rededication of the Holy Temple after Judas Maccabaeus led his small band of "Maccabees" to military victory over Antiochus IV.

This "Festival of Lights" is celebrated for eight days. On the first night, one candle is lit in a candelabrum called a "menorah." On the second day, two candles are lit, and so on. This is to celebrate the fact that a tiny drop of oil kept the "eternal light" of the temple burning for eight whole days.

**Materials Needed**
paper, scissors, small pencil

**Time Required**
1 hour

**In The End**
Child will create a dreidel for grandparent

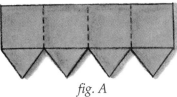

fig. A

Jewish children play the traditional dreidel game during Hanukkah.
A dreidel is a little toy top. You can help your child make his own dreidel. Cut out the body and cover shapes as shown (fig. A), and fold along dotted lines. Draw a grid of 2" squares on a piece of paper. Draw one Hebrew letter on each of the cover flaps (fig. B).

Shin  Nun  Hay  Gimel

fig. B

The letters *nun, gimel, hay* and *shin* stand for the words "Nes gadol haya sham," or "A great miracle happened there." Tape the dreidel together and insert a small pencil through the center to create both the handle and point of the dreidel.

To play the game, each player starts with an equal amount of gelt (chocolate coins). You may use jelly beans, nuts, or pennies. The same amount is placed in a center pile. Each player spins in turn and does one of the following, based on which letter is facing up after his spin: **Nun** = nothing; **Gimel** = Take all of the pile; **Shin** = Add two pieces to the pile; **Hay** = Get half of the pile. The player who ends up with everything wins.

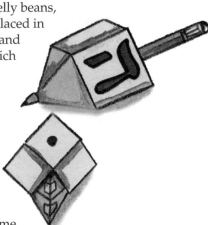

Send a dreidle to your child's grandparent along with the instructions for the game. He and your child can play together, over the phone if necessary. They can play game after game and have a lot of fun.

# SILENT NIGHT

● ● ● ● ● ● ● ● ● ● ● ● ● ●

**Materials Needed**
pen & paper

**Time Required**
1 hour

**In The End**
Child will share the Christmas story with his grandparent in a new way

## OTHER IDEAS

◆

Have your child write his story in book format with a few lines on each page accompanied by illustrations.

We are all familiar with the song whose lyrics describe a silent and holy night. All was calm and bright. That night, of course, was the first Christmas. The images created in many of the songs for Christmas are those of peace, glory and reverence.

Songs help to paint a picture of how that night was, but to develop a clearer picture, it is helpful to give some thought to the actual events surrounding the birth of Christ as written in the New Testament in Luke, chapter two.

A meaningful way for your child to get a feel for that special birthday is to have him write a short story assuming the role of one of the key characters. Have him pretend that he was actually there and write about his experience. He can choose his role from the following list or think of one on his own. He can be:

- an animal in the stable
- the bright star in the sky
- a shepherd in the field
- Mary's donkey
- an angel
- the innkeeper
- a sheep in the field
- Joseph or Mary

After the story is written, send a copy of it to your child's grandparent. He has likely never heard the story told in that way and it will surely enrich his understanding of the Christmas story.

# SPECIAL SEDAR PLATE

The Jewish celebration of Passover reminds us of the time when the Jews were slaves in Egypt and God freed them after sending ten plagues to the land to demonstrate his sovereignty to the Pharaoh. When the Angel of Death came to kill the first born child of the Egyptians, he passed over the homes of the Jewish children, whose families had faith in God.

The ceremonial Passover dinner is called a "sedar," which means "order." Throughout the course of the sedar, the story of the Passover is told and the participants eat foods that remind them of that time of oppression in Egypt followed by freedom and thanks to God.

Your child can create his own sedar plate. Onto a paper plate, have him glue construction paper items that look like the following foods:

- **Matzo -** "The bread of affliction," unleavened bread like the Jews must have eaten in the desert when they had to keep walking and had no time for their bread to rise. Jewish people refrain from eating any leavened food, such as bread, during the eight-day holiday of Passover.

- **Charoses -** Apple, cinnamon and wine mixture that resembles the mortar that was used by the slaves to lay bricks.

- **Horseradish -** Bitter herbs to remember bitter times of slavery.

- **Egg & Parsley-** Resembles the miracle of new life.

- **Lamb's Bone -** Used to mark the doors of the jews so the Angel of Death knew to pass over.

The moral of the Passover story is the deliverance of the faithful people by God. Have your child and his grandparent discuss something in their lives from which God delivered them or a time that they demonstrated faith and were rewarded for it.

**Materials Needed**
paper plate, construction paper, glue, scissors

**Time Required**
1 hour

**In The End**
Child will create a sedar plate for his grandparent and both will discuss the importance of faith

## OTHER IDEAS

Let your child decorate a paper cup to be used as the special wine cup for the sedar.

# RIBBON WREATH

## OTHER IDEAS

◆

The custom of decorating with greenery at Christmastime is based on an ancient custom. Long ago, even before Christianity, the evergreens were greatly valued, partly because they held the promise of spring and new life. Because Christ holds the promise of life for Christians, it is fitting to decorate with evergreens for his birthday.

Evergreen branches and boughs are used to decorate in many ways. One of the most traditional ways to display them is in the form of a wreath: a circle with no beginning and no end. Your child can make a wreath that is guaranteed to always stay green. He will need an embroidery hoop or a piece of hanger wire bent into a circle and fastened. He will also need a lot of green ribbon or thick yarn cut into pieces that are three inches long.

To create the wreath, he will simply tie each piece of ribbon onto the circular form. One at a time, side by side, the ribbons should be tied all around the circle. When finished, the wreath can be sent to his grandparent to remind her of God's promise of new life in Christ. Life that is eternal and has no end.

# GREAT GROGGERS

The Jewish celebration of Purim is an especially fun one for children. It is a festival that celebrates the deliverance of the Jews in ancient Persia.

The story of a very brave man named Mordecai can be found in the Bible in the book of Esther. He believed in God and therefore refused to bow down to Haman, the man who was second to King Ahasuerus. This infuriated Haman and he asked the king to murder all of the Jews. Mordecai's sister, Esther, was the wife of the king. Together, Mordecai and Esther turned the tables on Haman and saved the Jews in the town of Shusan. They bravely stood up for what they knew was right.

It is this victory that is celebrated on Purim. The holiday is marked by a boisterous costume party during which children dress up like characters from the Purim story. The children all hold "groggers," loud noisemakers, and the Purim story is told to the group. At every mention of the mean Haman, the children shake their groggers and yell, "Boo!" Everyone eats fruit-filled cookies called hamantashen, which are triangular like Haman's hat. A grand time is had by all.

Have your child think about a time when he stood up for what he knew was right despite opposition. He can document the event in a note to his grandparent and thank her for any role she may have had in teaching him to stand up for what he believes.

**Materials Needed**
pen & paper

**Time Required**
20 minutes

**In The End**
Child will thank grandparent for helping to build her character

## OTHER IDEAS

◆

To help your child make a grogger, simply place some dry beans between two sturdy paper plates. Staple the plates together all the way around. Let your child decorate the noisemaker with markers, paint and glitter.

# LIGHT OF THE WORLD

**Materials Needed**
Styrofoam balls, sequins, tiny straight pins, ribbon

**Time Required**
1 1/2 hours

**In The End**
Child will make sparkly ornaments for himself and his grandparent

## OTHER IDEAS

◆

Create ornaments by covering Styrofoam balls with glue and wrapping yarn or ribbon all around them.

◆

Create candy cane ornaments by threading red and white beads onto pipe cleaners, bending them into a cane shape.

One starry Christmas Eve, the German minister Martin Luther, went for a walk outside through the evergreen trees. He felt like he could see the stars shining on the icy trees, and wanted to share this with his whole family. He cut down a small fir tree, brought it home and decorated it with small candles to look like stars. He said the glowing tree stood for Christ who is the Light of the World. Also, evergreen trees are always green and represent the eternal life given through Christ. The Christmas tree is a tradition that has spread all over the world and fills the holiday with joy and light.

Just as Martin Luther found a way to share with his family the beauty he saw, so your child can share the beauty of a Christmas tree with his grandparent. Let him make some sparkly ornaments to adorn his grandparent's tree.

Purchase some Styrofoam balls and tiny straight pins at a craft store. Let your child cover the entire surface of the ball with colored sequins. Each sequin can be attached to the ball with a tiny pin. The finished effect is a beautiful ball that sparkles and shines. Attach a loop of ribbon to the top of the ball with a pin so that the ornament can hang from the boughs of a tree.

Your child can make similar ornaments for himself and his grandparent. In this way, the two can feel a special connection when they look at that ornament and know that it's "twin" hangs on the tree of the other.

# ADVENT TREE

• • • • • • • • • • • • • • • •

**A**dvent is a word based on the Latin word *adventus* which means "coming" or "arrival." Christians use the word advent to refer to the season before Christmas. It includes four Sundays. The time of advent should be observed as a season of meditation and preparation for Christmas, but it is also an exciting time. It is helpful to have a calendar that keeps track of the days of advent.

Your child can make an "advent tree" to serve this purpose for his grandparent. Have him cut a tree shape out of large piece of green construction paper or poster board. Next, he should cut out 25 little paper "ornaments" for the tree in the shapes of symbols of the season, (lambs, angels, stars, doves, bells, hearts, trumpets and the like).

Place the ornaments in an envelope and send them, with the paper tree, to his grandparent. Instruct his grandparent to tape one ornament to the tree each day leading up to Christmas. When the last ornament is placed, it will be Christmas day and your child's fully decorated tree will make his grandparent's Christmas very special.

**Materials Needed**
paper, scissors, construction paper

**Time Required**
2 hours

**In The End**
Child will create an advent tree to build Christmas excitement for his grandparent

## OTHER IDEAS

◆

Let your child make a special star for the top of the advent tree. It can be decorated with glitter or a meaningful Bible verse.

# METAMORPHOSIS

## OTHER IDEAS

◆

**Study other animals whose bodies change during their life cycle and think of fun ways to create crafty versions of those animals.**

Various organisms change their form during their life cycle. For example, long-tailed tadpoles turn into frogs. Caterpillars turn into beautiful butterflies.

Humans do not change in form like frogs or butterflies, but we do grow and change throughout the course of our lives. Certain events mold us into the adults we grow up to be. As we experience different things, we see the world in different ways.

One of the most exciting changes in a person's life happens when they get to know God. A metamorphosis occurs within that person, and suddenly the world is a much more beautiful and wondrous place. Just as a caterpillar becomes something of great beauty after its metamorphosis is complete, so people receive an inner peace and beauty once they know God.

Let your child make a butterfly to illustrate this transformation. Fold a coffee filter several times and dip each corner into some watered-down paint. Let the paint soak into the filter. Unfold. Once dry, fold the filter back and forth, as if you were making a paper fan. Pinch it together in the center and fasten it with a clothespin. Paint or glue eyes onto the clothespin and attach some pipe cleaners bent into the shape of antennae to the pin. The resulting butterfly can be glued to a magnet and displayed on the refrigerator of your child's grandparent, who will be reminded of the beautiful transformation his grandchild has undergone from a little baby to a child with knowledge of God.

# MANGER MOBILE

Your child can create a mobile incorporating all of the characters of the Christmas story. Each piece will be made of homemade dough and hung from a wire hanger by strings of various lengths.

The dough recipe and procedure are as follows:

- Combine 4 cups of all-purpose flour, 1 cup of salt and 1 1/2 cups of water

- Knead until dough forms

- Roll dough out and create shapes with cookie cutters, or by bending and molding pieces of dough

- Place dough figures on a baking sheet

- Use a drinking straw to create a hole near the top of each figure

- Bake dough figures in a 325° oven for 45 minutes

- Allow ornaments to cool completely before painting them with acrylic paints

- Allow paint to dry completely and spray figures with polyurethane glaze

Encourage your child to create figures such as angels, a star, Mary, Joseph, baby Jesus in the manger, and animals. Once the figures are done, tie strings to them and tie the strings to the hanger to create a mobile. Give some thought to the length of the strings. For example, use a short string for the star and angels so they will float higher than the other figures.

Send the mobile to your child's grandparent.

**Materials Needed**
paint, flour, salt, water, straw, hanger, polyurethane glaze, string

**Time Required**
2 hours

**In The End**
Child will make a Christmas mobile for his grandparent

## OTHER IDEAS

◆

Make the figures out of paper.

# SABBATH REST

**Materials
Needed**
time only

**Time Required**
a few minutes
each week

**In The End**
Grandparent
and child will
spend precious
moments
together
each week in
observance of
the Sabbath

## OTHER IDEAS

◆

Encourage your
child and his
grandparent to
discuss ways
to incorporate
God and
worship into
the following
week.

**A**fter creating heaven and earth and everything within, God rested. He ended His work and blessed and sanctified the seventh day, setting it apart from the others as a day of rest. The Hebrew term *shabath*, meaning "to cease," has been assigned to this special day, the Sabbath.

God later commanded us to keep the Sabbath holy. It is a day set aside for Him. The Sabbath is observed in different ways by different people. Some people have rules as to exactly what you are allowed to do on that day, and exactly what is forbidden. One thing is constant: The Sabbath is God's day, and whatever we do or refrain from doing is secondary to the important purpose of focusing on Him.

Have your child take some time on the Sabbath to spend some quite moments alone with God. He can read from the Bible, say prayers, sing songs or just have a quiet thought or conversation. Let him start a ritual of speaking to his grandparent each Sabbath. They can chat about their respective weeks and share a prayer. This can become a special time that they both look forward to every week.

# A PLACE OF SHELTER

● ● ● ● ● ● ● ● ● ● ● ● ● ● ● ● ● ● ● ● ● ● ● ●

S ukkot, or "Feast of Tabernacles," is a Jewish festival that is celebrated in the autumn. It is a time when thanks is given for the year's harvest. In ancient times, when the farmers would go out in the fields to harvest their crops, they built little temporary booths for shelter. They would sleep in the little booths whose roofs, if existent, were made of twigs and were so thin that the starry sky could be seen right through them.

Today, Sukkot is celebrated by the building of a "sukkah," or little booth, much like those of old. They are made of twigs and are decorated with fruits and vegetables. Their purpose is to provide a place of shelter where one can gaze up to the heavens and be thankful for the bounty of the harvest.

Though your child need not build a sukkah, it is a nice idea to send her outside to have a quiet moment of thanks for the food she is lucky enough to have and for all other blessings. In the absence of a sukkah, she can sit on the grass and look up through the branches of a tree and give

some thought to all of the blessings she has to be thankful for.

Encourage her to list these things and to send the list to her grandparent with instructions for the grandparent to do the same activity. Upon receiving the grandparent's list, your child can know that she and her grandparent both shared a special time of quiet thanks to acknowledge everything with which they have been blessed.

**Materials Needed**
pen & paper
**Time Required**
1 hour
**In The End**
Child and grandparent will share thoughts of thankfulness

## OTHER IDEAS

Your child can cut out colorful paper fruits and vegetables and write something for which she is thankful on each one.

*Sacred Celebrations*
**131**

# NOAH'S ARK

● ● ● ● ● ● ● ● ● ● ● ● ● ●

**Materials Needed**
index card, pen, beads, string

**Time Required**
30 minutes

**In The End**
Child will establish a covenant with his grandparent

## OTHER IDEAS

◆

The animals boarded the ark two by two. Let your child and his grandparent reminisce about things they have done together— two by two.

**A**fter Noah's Ark made it through the great flood and God made the rains stop, Noah and his family saw a beautiful rainbow in the sky. The rainbow was a covenant between God and the people. It was God's promise that He would never again flood the entire earth. Every time we see a colorful rainbow in the sky, we are reminded of that promise. We know that God always keeps his promises, and it is reassuring to see a reminder of that across the sky after a rain.

Though we are only human, we can make promises to others and give them special reminders of those promises. Have your child make a special promise to his grandparent and write the promise down on an index card. For example, the card could read, "Grandpa, I promise to always love you forever and ever."

As a reminder of that promise, let your child string several colored beads onto a string, one bead for each color of the rain-bow. Tie the string together to create a bracelet. Your child can send the promise and the bracelet to his grandparent, establishing a special covenant between them.

# BIBLE BISCUITS

H ere is a fun recipe that your child can share with her grandparent. A Bible will be required to determine what ingredients are needed. Let your child copy the recipe and send it to her grandparent. Once the grandparent thinks he has the ingredients figured out, he can check them with your child to be sure they are correct. In so doing, the two will have a conversation based on verses of the Bible.

This recipe is so easy that your child and her grandparent can easily make these biscuits at their respective homes. They can then speak again to see how yummy they turned out.

The recipe for Bible Biscuits is as follows:

2 cups I Kings 4:22          1/2 cup Psalm 55:21
3 tsp. Amos 4:5              3/4 cup Lamentations 4:7
1/4 tsp. Leviticus 2:13

Combine I Kings, Amos and Leviticus. Cut the Psalm in until mixture resembles coarse crumbs. Add Lamentations. Knead 3-4 times. Roll dough to 3/4" thick and cut out 2" circles with a biscuit cutter or empty can. Bake on lightly greased cookie sheet at 450° for 10 minutes.

*Interpretation is:*

*2 cups flour*               *1/2 cup butter*
*3 tsp. baking powder*       *3/4 cup milk*
*1/4 tsp. salt*

## Materials Needed
Bible, ingredients

## Time Required
1 1/2 hours

## In The End
Grandparent and child will bake Bible Biscuits

# OTHER IDEAS

Search the Bible for other ingredients, such as almonds in Numbers 17:8. Devise your own recipes based on these ingredients.

# HOLIDAY JOURNAL

**Materials Needed**
empty journal
or spiral note-
book, pen

**Time Required**
a few minutes
after each
holiday

**In The End**
Child will give
thought to
the meaning
of holidays

## OTHER IDEAS

◆

Do not wait
for the end of
the year! After
each holiday is
celebrated and
its journal page
completed,
send a copy of
the page to
your child's
grandparent.
He will appreci-
ate the
thought given
to each special
day and will be
encouraged to
himself see the
significance in
the holidays.

As the seasons go by, we celebrate many holidays. Most of them are celebrated in a fun way and then forgotten until next year's celebration. These days, we often get so involved in planning fun parties and devising interesting ways to observe holidays that we forget the real reason for which the holiday exists.

An excellent example of this is Christmas. Each year, many people strive to have a Christmas that is bigger and better than the last. The true meaning of the holiday is often for-gotten, and the precious quiet moments with family are few and far between.

This year, have your child keep a holiday journal. After each holiday passes, urge him to write a page in his journal about how it was celebrated.

To continue with the example of Christmas, after the big day has come and gone, your child can record his memories of the events that preceded it as well as the day itself. Challenge him to put into words the feelings he felt while singing hymns or reading the first Christmas story in the Bible. He can write about the parties and activities, candy making, gift wrapping and decorating that were such a fun part of the Christmas preparation, but more important, he should write about what Christmas meant to him this year.

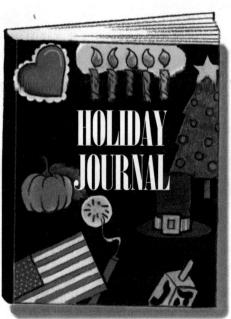

At the end of the year, your child can photocopy the pages of the journal to send to his grandparent. His grandparent will be very proud to see the depth at which his grandchild understands the holidays of the year.

# OUR DAILY BREAD

E very day is a gift from God. We must be careful to remember to say "Thank You" for all of our blessings on a daily basis. Even on days when we feel sad or angry, it is easy to look around and find something to be thankful for. Some families have traditional prayers of thanks before each meal. Some say bedtime prayers. Whatever the time of day, it is important to stop and give thanks where it is due.

One of the most important things to be thankful for is our family. How wonderful it would be to incorporate thanks for family into the daily blessing before the meal. Let your child make up a prayer that accomplishes this. For example; "A,B,C,D,E,F,G. Thank you, God, for feeding me. H, I, J, K, L-M-N-O-P. Thank you for my family." The blessing can be as long or as short, as fun or as serious as your child wants it to be.

Challenge your child to incorporate into the prayer a special thanks for grandparents who may live in a different place and cannot share the meal with you. Write the prayer on a piece of paper, and send it in the mail to the grandparent so that he will know that he is remembered in the prayers of his grandchild.

**Materials Needed**
pencil & paper
**Time Required**
15 minutes
**In The End**
Child will write a blessing of thanks for things in his life, including his grandparent

## OTHER IDEAS

◆

Designate one day a week to go around the table and take turns telling each family member that you are thankful for them and state at least one thing you like about them. Do the same for the grandparent who is not present, and write that down in a note to be sent in the mail.

# HONOR THY GRANDPARENTS

**Materials Needed**
pen & paper

**Time Required**
45 minutes

**In The End**
Child will refer to the Bible for life instructions

## OTHER IDEAS

◆

Help your child make a bookmark with the verse from Exodus 20:12. Use it to mark a special place in your family Bible or your child's Bible.

Honor your father and mother, that your days may be long upon the land which the Lord your God is giving you.
Exodus 20:12

The Bible is very clear as to how we are to regard our parents. This is true for grandparents, too. In Biblical times, families usually lived together on the same land for generation after generation. Grandparents were a vital part of the family dynamic, participating in farming and child rearing.

Today's lifestyles are different. We rarely live with our grandparents, but that does not change our responsibility to them in God's eyes. We simply must use different methods to show them our love and respect.

All of the activities in this book are means toward the same end of sharing love with and, essentially, "honoring" your child's grandparent. Set aside a quiet few minutes one day and sit down with your child and a Bible. Help him to locate the Ten Commandments and to understand their importance. Explain that they are rules for us to live our lives by and that they are not to be broken. Stress the importance of parents and grandparents and look up the word "honor" in the dictionary. Help your child list on a piece of paper all the ways he can honor his grandparent, even from afar.

Encourage your child to keep the list in a special place in his room so he can refer to it as often as he needs to. Help him every day to remember to demonstrate what he has learned.

# JUST BECAUSE
# I LOVE YOU

# LIVE & LEARN

● ● ● ● ● ● ● ● ● ● ● ● ● ●

**Materials Needed**
paper & pen, grandparent

**Time Required**
20 minutes for child, 20 minutes for grandparent

**In The End**
Grandparent will encourage child in her studies and validate the need for school

## OTHER IDEAS

Challenge your child to think of some things she is not being taught in school that she thinks would be helpful for her to know.

**E**very child has moments during her education when she questions the necessity of learning certain things. It may seem ridiculous to have to memorize the Pythagorean Theorem or dissect a frog. She may question her need to know how to figure out the circumference of a circle or to diagram a sentence. With her limited experience, it can be hard to imagine the need for such knowledge.

Her grandparent has lived longer and, naturally, is much wiser. The next time your child seems discouraged by the things she is being required to learn, have her discuss it with her grandparent. Let her make a list of knowledge she deems frivolous. Send it to her grandparent with a request to explain ways in which that kind of knowledge will be needed later in life. Her grandparent can write back with the explanations.

Admittedly, some things our children are required to know seemingly defy explanation, but most of the things they are learning will somehow help them later. It will probably be reassuring for your child to have it on good authority that all of her hard work now will have its reward in the future.

SPELLING

LITERATURE

# SURFING THE NET

Scavenger hunts are fun activities during which teams of people each have a list of items that can be found in a home. Each team races to see which one can find all of the items on the list by going door to door and asking neighbors if they have anything on the list. The first team to get all of the items is the winner.

Your child and her grandparent can go on a scavenger hunt for information on the Internet. Instead of having it be a race, have each one of them make a list of ten questions or items. They can dictate the lists to each other over the phone or mail, e-mail or fax them to each other. The point of the game will be for each of them to surf the Internet to learn as much as they can about the list of items the other made for them.

A sample list follows:

- What are fossils?
- How can you tell an Indian elephant from an African elephant?
- Why do birds have feathers?
- How do bees make honey?
- Where is the world's highest waterfall?
- What caused the Civil War?
- How does an earthquake happen?
- What is the sun made of?
- Why do stars twinkle?
- What causes an echo?

Feel free to use these questions or any others you can think of. Have your child and her grandparent download or write down their answers and share them with each other.

**Materials Needed**
paper & pen, computer

**Time Required**
2 hours

**In The End**
Child and grandparent will simultaneously increase their knowledge

## OTHER IDEAS

Make note of the Web sites visited during this activity for future reference.

# WAKE-UP CALL

● ● ● ● ● ● ● ● ● ● ● ● ● ● ●

**Materials Needed**
telephone

**Time Required**
A few minutes

**In The End**
Child and grand-parent will spend a few minutes together in the morning

The mood of your entire day can be set by the first thing you do in the morning. Have your child start his day by placing a phone call to his grandparent.

One morning, as soon as your child wakes up, have her pick up the phone and give a big "Good Morning" to her grand-parent. She may find her still in bed or already up and about. One thing is certain: She will definitely be pleased to hear the voice of her grandchild on the phone. Her day will no doubt contain more happiness and smiles as a result of that simple phone call.

Your child's day will be better, too, remem-bering the short greeting she shared with her grandparent first thing in the morning.

# OTHER IDEAS

Let your child place a "Good Night" call to her grandparent to end the day in a happy way.

# SCRATCH ART

● ● ● ● ● ● ● ● ● ● ● ● ● ● ● ● ● ● ● ●

B y now, your child has likely created countless pictures for his grandparent. Scratch art is a fun activity and results in a colorful picture unlike any regular crayon or marker drawing your child may have created in the past.

Your child must first use crayons to color over the entire surface of a piece of thick paper. The crayon should be used heavily, so he must apply a lot of pressure as he colors. Have him use many different colors, applying them randomly in little blotches about the size of a quarter. They must all overlap slightly, leaving no empty paper showing between them.

Once the paper is full of color, use a paint brush to apply a coat of very thick black poster paint. Several coats of black may be necessary to completely cover the waxy crayon. Be sure to let each coat dry completely before adding another.

When the paper is dry and completely black, the fun can really begin. Give your child a toothpick and let him begin "drawing" with it on the black paper. As he presses the toothpick down to draw his picture, he will be scratching off the black paint to reveal the color beneath. The result is a picture whose every line is comprised of several colors.

Send the finished picture to your child's grandparent who will certainly appreciate its unique style.

**Materials Needed**
thick paper, crayons, black poster paint, toothpick

**Time Required**
1 1/2 hours

**In The End**
Child creates a picture for grandparent in an unusual way

## OTHER IDEAS

❧

Black crayon can be used instead of poster paint. It is more time consuming to cover all of the colors using a black crayon, but it can certainly be done.

# PRAYER ROCK

**Materials Needed**
small rock, fabric, index card, ribbon, hole punch

**Time Required**
35 minutes

**In The End**
Child will send grandparent a poem and prayer rock

A nice way to end each day is to say a little prayer. The prayer can be one of thanks for the blessings in your life or a request for a special blessing for your loved ones. It can include anything that you want it to. Your child can add a prayer to his bedtime routine and it will likely become a time he looks forward to each night.

Remind him to mention thanks for his grandparent in his nightly prayer. Have him make a "prayer rock" for his grandparent to make him a part of this prayer routine, as well.

All he needs to do is go outside and find a small rock with a nice, smooth shape. He can cut a piece of fabric into a circle about 4" in diameter, place the rock in the center of it and wrap the fabric up around the rock. Tie it closed with a ribbon to create a little bundle with the rock inside. Next, he can copy the following poem onto an index card and punch a hole in one corner of the card. Thread the ribbon through the hole and tie the card onto the bundle.

The poem follows:

*I made this little prayer rock*
*And sent it right to you*
*To place beneath your pillow*
*So when your day is through*
*Your head will lay to slumber*
*And feel the rock down there*
*To serve as a reminder*
*To say a little prayer.*
*Please know that every evening*
*I will be praying, too*
*Among the things I'll mention*
*Is how thankful I am for you.*

Send the rock with the poem to your child's grandparent. When placed beneath his pillow, the rock will serve as a reminder to the grandparent that prayers are said for him by his grandchild. The nightly tradition you start is sure to bring joy to them both.

# MORAL OF THE STORY

**W**hile some stories are written merely to entertain, those classified as "fables" always have a moral. The "moral of the story" is the lesson the reader learns about correct behavior and good character.

Explain to your child the definition and intent of a fable, encouraging him to write one of his own to send to his grandparent. You may want to remind him of a fable that he knows; for example, the legendary story of the tortoise and the hare from which we learn the lesson "slow and steady wins the race."

If he is not familiar with any fables, go to the library where you can find books full of them. He will likely notice that most fables feature animals which act like humans and serve as the main characters in the stories.

It is important for him to decide on the moral of his story before your child begins writing his own fable. Have him think back on lessons he has learned lately about life. Since he will be sending the fable to his grandparent, it would be especially meaningful to feature a lesson he learned from his grandparent. Maybe his grandparent has taught him something merely by example, like "laughter is the best medicine" or "time heals all wounds."

When the story is finished, have your child write the moral at the end of the story, ("...and the moral of the story is... ") Send it to his grandparent, who will be touched to realize that she has taught her grandchild a valuable life lesson.

### Materials Needed
paper & pen, imagination

### Time Required
1 1/2 hours

### In The End
Grandparent will receive a story with a moral that she instilled in her grandchild

## OTHER IDEAS

❈

Fold some pieces of paper together and staple them at the fold to create a little book for your child to write his story in. Encourage him to illustrate it as well.

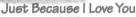

*Just Because I Love You*

# JOINT EFFORT

● ● ● ● ● ● ● ● ● ● ● ● ● ● ● ● ●

**Materials Needed**
paper & pen, watercolors, crayons, or colored pencils

**Time Required**
1 hour total

**In The End**
Child and Grandparent will write and illustrate a poem together

## OTHER IDEAS

✿

Instead of a poem, have one participant write lyrics to a song and the other one compose a melody for it. They can tape the songs and entertain each other.

**A**lthough it is certainly wonderful for your child's grandparent to receive an item in the mail that her grandchild has created, it is even more meaningful for her to be able to help in its creation. A good activity for the two to pursue together is the writing and illustration of a poem.

Instruct them each to write a poem. The poems can be about anything they choose. They can talk about it and decide on the subjects together, or each decide on her own. The only thing they should keep in mind is that a poem is, by definition, designed to convey a vivid and imaginative sense of experience through the use of the words in its verses.

When each of them has composed their respective poem, they should send it to the other for the second phase of the activity. Illustration: Each participant will read the poem the other has written. After thinking about what kinds of images it inspires, each should do his best to create that image on paper.

They can use watercolor or crayon, pen or pencil. The medium they use is not as important as the content of their picture. When they are finished with the pictures, each participant should mail the poem along with its illustration back to the poet.

Both child and grandparent will learn something about the other by participating in this activity of writing and drawing. They will both certainly be pleased with the finished work.

# BEANS & PEAS

● ● ● ● ● ● ● ● ● ● ● ● ● ● ● ● ● ● ●

Not only are dried beans and peas an excellent source of food, they are also wonderful art supplies. It is great fun to create a mosaic using the colorful little seeds.

Traditionally, a mosaic is a decorative picture, designed by setting small colored pieces of rock, glass or tile in mortar. Since a picture made of rock and mortar would cost a fortune to mail to her grandparent, your child can create a mosaic using glue and dried beans and peas.

Purchase a bag of assorted dried beans and peas at the grocery store. It will probably cost less than a dollar. Give your child a piece of posterboard which has been cut down to 8" x 10" to eventually fit nicely into an envelope.

The child can draw a picture on the paper and instead of coloring the picture with crayons or markers, have her glue colorful beans onto the paper to create a colorful mosaic. Pictures with large areas to be colored are much easier to do in this technique than are pictures with small details. Large flowers or trees, animals or abstract designs work very well.

When finished, the mosaic can be sent to your child's grandparent. In ancient Greece, mosaics were often created on the walls of bathrooms. Perhaps your child's grandparent will want to display his new mosaic in his bathroom!

## Materials Needed
dried beans and peas, glue, posterboard

## Time Required
1 hour

## In The End
Child will create a mosaic for her grandparent

# OTHER IDEAS

❀

Thoroughly clean and save egg shells after you use eggs. When you have a dozen or so collected, let your child paint them different colors and then break them into pieces about 1/2" large. The colorful little shell fragments make beautiful mosaics, their irregular shapes lending a very authentic mosaic look.

# CUT A RECORD

● ● ● ● ● ● ● ● ● ● ● ● ● ● ● ●

## OTHER IDEAS

❀

Cut a piece of paper down to the size of the paper "cover" in the tape case. Have your child draw or write on the paper to create a visually interesting cover for his tape. Instead of drawing a picture, he may find a photo in a magazine and cut it down to fit in the case.

Does your child like rock and roll music or country western? Classical, rap or rhythm and blues? Music is an art and is intended to elicit an aesthetic response in its listener. It is universal in its appeal and is a part of the lives of almost every person in the world. We listen to music on our radios and primitive tribes across the globe chant rhythmic melodies.

Expressive in its nature, music tells a lot about its composer and creator. Your child might express himself with music by making up songs or tapping out tunes on a table with a pencil. Have him pretend to be a professional musician and cut a record of his own to send to his grandparent.

Give him a tape recorder and a tape and leave the rest to him. He can sing songs he likes or create songs of his own. Encourage him to use musical instruments if he has any, or to create some if he does not. Pots and pans or empty oatmeal boxes make excellent drums. Coffee cans half filled with rice or pebbles make great maracas.

When the tape is finished, send it to his grandparent. Your grandchild may not win a Grammy, but he will most likely become the favorite musical artist of his grandparent.

# PRECIOUS MOMENTS

Our family lives are filled with precious moments. It would be nice if your child's grandparent were there to witness a lot more of them. Since he likely feels the same way, include the grandparent in some of these events with the aid of a video camcorder.

Keep your camcorder charged and in a readily accessible place so that when a "precious moment" happens, you can capture it on film. You may want to take the camera to your child's ballet recital or softball game, school music program or play.

Don't forget to film everyday events, as those are the ones that will mean so much to your child's grandparent. Film your child reading a book to his teddy bear or coloring a picture. Catch her fixing her hair or helping frost cupcakes. If your child receives a letter or present from her grandparent, videotape her opening it and her reaction to it.

Continue to add footage to the tape, and every once in a while send the tape in a padded envelope to your child's grandparent. After viewing it, he can send it back and you can continue to add to it. Before long, you will have filled an entire tape with precious memories that your child's grandparent will now be able to share.

**Materials Needed**
camcorder and video tape

**Time Required**
A few minutes here and there

**In The End**
Child will share daily events with her grandparent

## OTHER IDEAS

Have your child's grandparent film his daily events and send the tape to your child.

# HOMEMADE PAPER ART

**Materials Needed**
paper, water, slotted spoon, blender, framed screen (fine screen sandwiched between two wooden frames, fastened tightly together)

**Time Required**
2 hours

**In The End**
Child will learn a paper-making process while creating art for her grandparent

## OTHER IDEAS

❁

Place some leaves, pressed flowers or glitter on the screen before pouring on the pulp. They will become a part of the surface of the paper.

**Y**our child can recycle some old paper and create a piece of homemade paper of her own. The paper will be a work of art in itself, or can be written or drawn on, cut or painted to make a completely original piece of art for her grandparent.

Take some used paper (newspaper, printer paper, construction paper, etc.), and let your child tear it into small pieces. Place the paper pieces in a large bowl and fill the bowl with water. Let the paper soak for a few hours or overnight.

Next, use a slotted spoon to scoop out the paper pieces, which should be quite "fluffy-looking," as they are breaking down in the water, and place them in a blender. Add a cup of water to the blender, and blend for a minute until you have created a "paper pulp soup."

Place the framed screen in a sink and pour the paper pulp soup onto it. The water should run right through and the pulp should remain on the screen. Lightly press down on the screen with a large sponge to push a bit of the excess water out of the pulp into the sink below.

Remove the screen from the sink and place it on a thick stack of newspaper. Use the sponge to press down on the pulp. This will spread the pulp out, forcing it to cover the entire screen right up to the frame. It will also flatten it and absorb some of the excess water. Squeeze out the sponge over the sink to dry it out and repeat the pressing process until no more water is being absorbed. Place the entire screen on a wire rack to dry. When it is dry, peel your dried paper out of the frame.

# CRAYON MELTDOWN

Grandchildren can be a great help in the kitchen. Since your child may not be present in his grandparent's kitchen every time his help is needed, have him create a special dish towel for his grandparent to use. That way, his towel can be of service even when he is not there.

Let your child use crayons to write or draw anything he wants to on a plain cotton (not terry cloth) dish towel. His drawing can be decorative or representational. He can create a pattern, or write a message or his name. No matter how he chooses to decorate, have him press down rather hard with the crayons to apply a nice, thick amount of wax to the towel.

When he is finished, place the towel, colored side down, on a very thick stack of newspaper. Using the "cotton" setting, run the iron back and forth over the towel, applying pressure to the iron the entire time and being careful not to scorch the towel.

Allow the towel to cool and send it to your child's grandparent who will enjoy using it in her kitchen. The crayon design is fairly permanent, but to keep the colors at their brightest it is best to advise the grandparent to wash the towel in cool water.

**Materials Needed**
cotton dish towel, crayons, newspaper, iron

**Time Required**
1 hour

**In The End**
Child will create a dish towel to help his grandparent in the kitchen

## OTHER IDEAS

❖

Use the crayon-melt technique to decorate T-shirts, handkerchiefs, socks or other cotton garments.

# MARK YOUR PLACE

**Materials Needed**
construction paper, crayons or markers, scissors, hole punch, yarn

**Time Required**
30 minutes

**In The End**
Child will create a bookmark for his grandparent

## OTHER IDEAS

Have the bookmark laminated to make it more durable.

**M**any people enjoy sitting down with a good book to relax after a hard day. If your child's grandparent is one of these people, let your child make a special bookmark to send to his grandparent.

Cut some long rectangles, approximately 1 1/4" wide by 6" long, out of construction paper. Punch a hole near the top of the bookmark and tie a piece of yarn through it for a decorative tassel. The yarn will hang out of the top of the book, making it easier to find the exact page the reader was on when the book was left. As an alternative to the yarn, you can simply fold down the top inch of the bookmark creating a way for it to "hook onto" the top of a page.

Of course, the bookmark will function just as well without a tassel or a fold. It is purely a matter of preference.

Once the bookmark is cut out, let your child decorate it however she wants to using crayons or markers.

### SOME IDEAS...

- Glue a photo of your child or family pet onto the bookmark.

- Include a favorite Bible verse or quote; illustrate it, too!

- Use pictures that have been cut out of magazines to decorate the bookmark.

- Glue pressed flowers or leaves to the bookmark. Allow the glue to dry, then cover the entire bookmark with clear contact paper and trim it to the exact size of the bookmark. This will prevent the leaves or flowers from falling off.

- Write the title of your child's favorite book on the bookmark. Have him decorate it by illustrating his favorite part of the book.

# GETTING PUZZLED

● ● ● ● ● ● ● ● ● ● ● ● ● ● ● ● ● ● ● ● ● ●

**Materials Needed**
posterboard,
crayons,
markers,
scissors, glue,
magazines
(optional)

**Time Required**
35 minutes

**In The End**
Child will create
a puzzle for his
grandparent

Sometimes even adults get bored and long for something entertaining to do. Here's an idea for a quick project that will result in a fun puzzle for your child's grandparent.

Cut an 8" x 10" rectangle out of a piece of posterboard. Have your child draw a picture on it and color it in. Using a pair of scissors, cut the picture into several interestingly-shaped pieces, creating a puzzle. Put all of the pieces into an envelope and send it to your child's grandparent.

For other variations on this theme . . .

• Paint the picture instead of drawing

• Use rubber stamps or finger stamps to create the picture

• Use photos to create the picture

• Cut out pictures from a magazine and glue them onto the poster board to create the picture

• Have a photo of your child made into an 8" x 10" and cut it up to create the puzzle

## OTHER IDEAS

Decorate both
sides of the
posterboard
for a more
challenging,
two-sided
puzzle.

# WORD HUNT

**Materials Needed**
dictionary, paper, pen

**Time Required**
35 minutes

**In The End**
Child and grandparent will help each other increase their vocabulary

## OTHER IDEAS

❀

Upon receiving his grandparent's list of words, have your child write a letter to her grandparent, incorporating as many of the newly learned vocabulary words as possible.

The development of a large vocabulary is an ongoing process. There is no end to it, and we continue to add words to our vocabulary throughout our entire life. Sometimes, we learn words by association with other words or we hear them and are prompted to learn their meaning. Seldom do we take the time to sit down with a dictionary and make a conscious effort to learn new words.

This activity will prompt your child and her grandparent to motivate each other to learn some new words. They will each need a dictionary, some paper, a pen and an open mind. Their assignment is to first be a student, then a teacher and then a student again.

Each one of them should do the same thing. First, open the dictionary to the "A" section. Find a word that she does not know the meaning of and whose definition would lend it to become a part of her vocabulary in the future. Write down the word and its definition. Do the same thing for every letter of the alphabet. When finished, photocopy the list and send a copy to the other participant.

When each of them receive the other's list of words, they should study them and do their best to use some of the new words in their everyday vocabulary.

# SPECIAL REQUESTS

# SUMMER BOOK BUDDIES

**Materials Needed**
construction paper & pen, scissors

**Time Required**
A few minutes after each book

**In The End**
Child will have incentive to read books during the summer

## OTHER IDEAS

Grandparent can tell his grandchild which books he has read lately, and what they were about.

**S**ome schools and local libraries have summer reading programs to motivate kids to read while they are not in school.

To help your child maintain his excitement about reading throughout the summer, assign him a reading buddy—his grandparent. By having his grandparent involved in a summer reading program, your child will be especially motivated to read a lot of books. His grandparent will be thrilled to receive regular updates of his grandchild's reading efforts.

Have your child actually create a work of art for his grandparent by reading books. At the beginning of the summer, have your child think of some kind of picture that can be constructed with different parts. Each part will be cut out of colored construction paper and will contain the name of a book that has been read by your child.

For example, your child may want to do a train or a caterpillar, a bouquet of flowers or a starry sky. Each time your child reads a book, he will create a piece of the picture, (for example: a train car, segment of the caterpillar, flower blossom or star), write the name of the book on it and send it to his grandparent. His grandparent will start to assemble the picture and add parts to it each time they are received.

At the end of the summer, the grandparent can send the finished picture back to the child or take a photograph of himself standing next to it. Your child will enjoy seeing the completed picture, and his grandparent will enjoy being a part of the process and learning what kinds of books his grandchild has been reading.

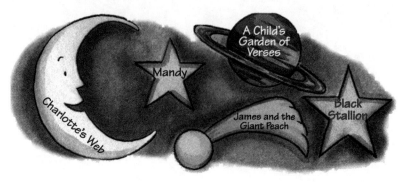

# BOOK REPORTER

●●●●●●●●●●●●●●●●●●●●●●●●

**Materials Needed**
pen & paper

**Time Required**
1 hour

**In The End**
Child will do a fun book report, grandparent will learn about the kinds of books his grandchild likes to read

**B**ook reports. We all had to do them during our school days. Some of us loved them. Some of us hated them. Inevitably, the books that we really wanted to read were not the ones which we had to write reports about. For some reason that we did not understand, the really exciting, fun to read books were not the ones our teachers wanted us to report on.

Give your child the opportunity to do a book report about a book that she has read "just for fun." Despite the fact that her teacher may not find them educational, some books are simply light and entertaining reading. These books are the ones that your child would love to actually do a report on, and who better to read and "grade" the report than your child's grandparent.

The next time your child reads a book that is not on the required reading list at school, let her do a fun report in any format she chooses. A list of ideas of book report formats:

- Illustrate a new cover for the book, and include a written "book review" on the back cover

- Pretend to interview a character from the book

- Assume the role of a character and write the report in the first person

- Videotape a short news report about the book

- Pretend to be the author and describe your intent with the book and things you would do differently if you had it to do over again

## OTHER IDEAS

Let your child do a science project "just for fun."

Send the finished book report to your child's grandparent. He will love to hear about one of his grandchild's favorite books.

# WISH I MAY, WISH I MIGHT

**Materials Needed**
pen & paper

**Time Required**
20 minutes

**In The End**
Child & grand-parent will share their wishes

## OTHER IDEAS

Throw a new light on the "wish scenario" by stipulating the following: "Any wish your child is granted, his worst enemy will receive twofold." Do the wishes change? In what way?

Wishing on the first star of the evening is an age old tradition. Receiving three wishes from a genie in a bottle is a concept often found in stories, in books or on television. Although we do not really believe that our wishes will be granted by stars or genies, it is fun to think about our wishes coming true.

We can learn a lot about a person by asking them what they would wish for if they were really going to be granted three wishes. Let your child ponder that question and send his answers to his grandparent.

Your child can write the wishes down and illustrate them if he wants to. He may want to write an imaginative story, or compose a poem or song about how he might come to be granted three wishes.

Whatever method he chooses, he will be forced to give some serious thought to his wishes. The grandparent will find out a lot about his grandchild by being told his wishes. He can then write down his wishes and send them to his grandchild. Who knows? They may share the same ones!

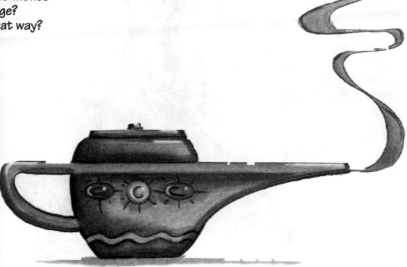

# FRAMED FOREVER

• • • • • • • • • • • • • • • • • • • • • • •

Your child's grandparent has received a lot of artwork from your child, and will continue to do so for quite some time. The refrigerator is a traditional gallery for children's artwork, and grandparents' refrigerators can become cluttered.

Have your child create a "frame" for his grandparent's refrigerator that can help reduce the clutter. This simple frame will become a constant in the ever-changing facade of the "grandparent refrigerator."

Glue two clothespins to the top of a piece of 9" x 12" corrugated board. The clothespins should be at the same level, both pointed down. They will be the clips that will hold on to the tops of future artwork.

Next, allow your child to decorate the board and clothespins any way she wants to. Supply paints and markers, glitter and glue, beads, buttons and pom-poms. She can attach baubles and bows, puzzle pieces, spiral noodles or ticket stubs to the border of the board. Let her be creative and imaginative in her decoration.

When finished, the frame will fit nicely in a postal priority envelope to be mailed to her grandparent. The frame can be taped to the refrigerator and will enjoy many years of assorted artwork.

**Materials Needed**
corrugated board, clothes-pins, decorative elements

**Time Required**
1 hour

**In The End**
Child will create a frame that his grandparent can use for years to come

# OTHER IDEAS

Create coordinating magnets by decorating individual clothespins and gluing them to magnetic tape. The pins can be used to hold photos or small items to display on the refrigerator or other metal surface.

# SECRET CODE

● ● ● ● ● ● ● ● ● ● ● ● ● ● ● ● ● ● ●

**Materials Needed**
pen & paper

**Time Required**
1 hour

**In The End**
Child will write a code letter to her grandparent

## OTHER IDEAS

Look up "Morse code" in the dictionary. It will likely have a picture of the patterns which represent the letters of the alphabet as designed by Samuel Morse for use over the wire telegraph. This is an example of an internationally recognized code and can be used by your child to create his code letter. In this way, he and his grandparent will be educating themselves about this famous code not often used by the average person.

It is not uncommon for spies or military commanders to communicate in code. Codes are systems of symbols, letters or words which are given arbitrary meanings, and are intended to maintain secrecy in messages.

Instead of writing her grandparent a regular letter, have your child try her hand at creating a code letter. Basically, she should devise a code in which each letter of the alphabet is assigned a different letter, number, shape or symbol. Then, she writes a letter using the assigned symbols in the place of the actual letters of the alphabet.

A legend should be provided in a box at the bottom of the paper or on another piece of paper to explain the symbols for each letter. This way, the grandparent will not have to "crack" the code, but can easily interpret the letter.

Your child and his grandparent will enjoy this fun new way of communicating. It will be interesting for your child to write, and fun for his grandparent to read.

# YOU'VE GOT MAIL

While e-mail can be impersonal when substituted for other communication, if used properly it can bring people closer together. Your child and his grandparent can send notes back and forth to each other via e-mail and keep one another informed of daily occurrences.

One fun way they can interact together utilizing the convenience of e-mail is to co-author a story. Let your child have the first turn. Let him think of a title for a story and the first paragraph of the story. Have him e-mail that to his grandparent with instructions for her to add the next paragraph to the story.

Continue this back and forth correspondence each contributing the next paragraph in the story. The plot can be funny or serious, mysterious or adventurous. Since neither knows what the other will write next, it will always be an exciting challenge to develop the story line based on the immediately preceding paragraph.

When the story finally reaches a conclusion, they can print out the final version and each keep a copy of their original, co-authored story.

You've Got Mail

**Materials Needed**
computer, imagination

**Time Required**
a few minutes each session

**In The End**
Child and grandparent will write a story together

## OTHER IDEAS

■

Each participant can create illustrations for the story, copy them, and mail them to the other

■

Suggest that your child and his grandparent write a poem together using the back and forth e-mail technique. For an added challenge, stipulate that the poem must rhyme.

# HOW I SPENT MY VACATION

**Materials Needed**
spiral notebook, pen, various memorabilia, tape

**Time Required**
A few minutes every day of vacation

**In The End**
Child will create a vacation journal to share with his grandparent

## OTHER IDEAS

After the vacation is over, have your child make a list of the most memorable things about the vacation, (most fun day, best food eaten, longest stretch without going to the bathroom, funniest thing that happened, etc.)

Include your child's grandparent in your next family vacation. No, she does not have to be there with you. Your child can keep a vacation journal to send her after the vacation is over. His grandparent will feel as if she were there the whole time.

Purchase a spiral notebook at the onset of your next vacation. At the end of each day, challenge your child to write a description of the day's activities. In addition to a mere description, have him comment on the best and worst, most boring, most exciting and funniest moments of the day.

Have him collect vacation memorabilia such as postcards, hotel stationery, sea shells, fallen leaves and restaurant napkins. At the end of the vacation, he can tape all of that paraphernalia into the pages of the notebook, writing a caption of explanation for each item.

Upon receiving the vacation journal in the mail, your child's grandparent will feel as if she was a real part of her grandchild's vacation. In fact, she was. Not a day went by that her grandchild didn't think about his grandparent as he wrote in his vacation journal.

Dear Gramma,
We had a great time on the island. You would have loved the seagulls, and yesterday there were several dolphins playing in the waves outside of our hotel. One of them jumped up out of the →

# PICTURE DISKS

**I**nstead of sending your child's grandparent loose photographs of your child for her to put in her own frames,
let your child create a "picture disk" with one of the
photos. Not only will it save the grandparent from having
to frame the photo, it will also provide her with yet another
original craft made by his grandchild.

Find a picture of your child in which his face is just the
right size to center over the lid of a mason jar. Use the metal
lid to trace a circle around the face in the picture, and let
your child cut the picture down to this circular shape.

Let your child glue the photo to the lid and then insert the
lid into the metal rim, gluing it in place with the photo
facing out. He can decorate the edge of the rim with a
ribbon, tying it in a bow at the top of the circular lid.

This creates a little round frame which can be hung by its
ribbon and displayed anywhere. It would look great
hanging from a hook, suctioned to a window or dangling
from the rearview mirror in a car. Wherever it winds up, it
will certainly be looked at often and appreciated greatly.

**Materials
Needed**
picture of child,
mason jar lid
and rim, glue,
scissors,
ribbon

**Time Required**
35 minutes

**In The End**
Child will create
a little framed
picture for his
grandparent

## OTHER IDEAS

Instead of a
photo, insert
a handwritten
poem or bible
verse into the
lid to create an
inspirational
little
ornament.

# THE MAD SCIENTIST

## OTHER IDEAS

**Challenge your child to think of an invention which the world would have been better off without. Have him explain why.**

**Have your child research important inventions of his grandparent's day.**

In this technological age of computers and the Internet, it seems that there are products and services available to fill our every need. People have gained so much knowledge that almost nothing seems to be beyond our grasp.

Actually, there must have been a similar feeling of scientific and intelligent supremacy during the times of all major inventions and technological advancements. The introduction of electricity, telephones, airplanes, televisions, space travel and the like no doubt affected the world in much the same way as today's new "inventions."

Even with all of the progress that has been made and all of the technology at our disposal, there are still more things to be learned and invented. Many times, it is an average person who develops a simple idea that blossoms into a wonderful invention which changes the world.

Ask your child what invention he thinks the world needs today. Encourage him to give the invention a name and write a description of it on a piece of paper. Ask him to include a statement about how that invention would change the world. Have him do a drawing of the invention and send the drawing, along with the written information about his invention, to his grandparent.

Perhaps some day your child's vision will become a reality. For now, at least he has given some thought to a way he could change the world and has shared his idea with someone he loves.

# EVERYDAY HEROES

To some people, a hero is a person of superhuman strength and power, able to leap over tall buildings and stop speeding trains with his bare hands. Some people may consider certain sports figures or movie stars to be heroes. In fact, anyone who is noted for his courage or nobility of character and purpose can be considered a hero.

Although it may often seem that heroes these days are few and far between, your child can likely list several people he looks up to and admires. Have him write down the names of people he considers to be heroes. For each hero, ask him to include an explanation of why he admires him. Ask your child to write down ways he wishes to be like the heroes he listed. Have him also write down reasons for which he is glad he is not like the heroes.

After giving some thought to the subject of heroes, your child may be able to name some things he has done that may make him a hero in somebody else's eyes. Perhaps he helped an ailing neighbor by washing his car or stood up to his peers for something he really believed in even if it was an unpopular choice. Have him write down some reasons for which he hopes someone will admire him in the future.

Send all of this "hero talk" to your child's grandparent, whose list of heroes likely differs from his grandchild's. Or they may be surprised to find that their ideas about heroes are quite similar.

**Materials Needed**
pen & paper

**Time Required**
25 minutes

**In The End**
Child will share his thoughts about heroism with his grandparent

## OTHER IDEAS

Have your child make a medal of honor out of paper. He can write "You are my Hero" on it and decorate it with glitter and ribbons.

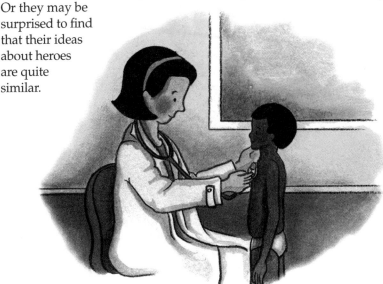

Special Requests
**163**

# COOKIE SWAP

**Materials Needed**
cookies, box, white tissue, index card

**Time Required**
2 hours

**In The End**
Child will send homemade cookies to his grandparent

## OTHER IDEAS

Have your child jot a note to his grandparent reminding him of a certain kind of cookie which he made for him in the past. He should mention how wonderful it would be if his grandparent would reciprocate this mailing with a batch of cookies sent to his grandchild!

There are few things in life as soothing as a batch of homemade cookies. The aroma that fills the house when the cookies are baking is second only to the love that is used to bake them.

Of course, a grandparent that does not live nearby rarely gets to partake in the yummy cookies baked by his grandchild. The next time your child helps in the kitchen to make a batch of homemade cookies, allow them to cool completely and then pack some up to send to his grandparent.

Empty oatmeal boxes or shoe boxes are wonderful for shipping cookies in. Be sure to wrap the delicious morsels in white tissue to prevent breakage. Include a letter or a drawing for an even more personal touch, and have your child write the cookie recipe on an index card in case his grandparent wants to bake a batch himself some day.

When he receives the tasty package in the mail, your child's grandparent will have both a full stomach and a happy heart.

# COUNT YOUR BLESSINGS

**Materials Needed**
pen & paper
**Time Required**
15 minutes
**In The End**
Child will realize how blessed he is to have a special grandparent, among so many other things

The expression "count your blessings" is used fairly often, but rarely is its meaning taken literally. Actually, people would probably feel a lot better about their lives if they took the literal meaning to heart.

When your child is feeling sad or sorry for herself, sit her down with a pen and a piece of paper. Have her list all of the blessings she has in her life. They may be large and important, like her good health, or seemingly insignificant, like her pet hamster. Instruct her not to finalize her list. It is ever growing, and she will likely think of more blessings to add to it on a regular basis.

After giving this matter some thought, whatever it was that was bothering your child should seem less significant compared to all of the wonderful things in her life. Let your child keep the list in a safe place in her room and refer to it any time she needs a little perspective.

Certainly, family members will be mentioned on your child's list. Have your child write a quick note to her grandparent to explain that she was literally counting her blessings and that having a loving grandparent was near the top of her list. This note will take only minutes for your child to write, and is guaranteed to be a very rich blessing in the life of her grandparent, who can reciprocate with a similar note to your child.

## OTHER IDEAS

Encourage your child to acknowledge other people on his list by sending them a quick note. From funny siblings to patient teachers, every person in her life to be told that he is a blessing will enjoy a feeling of pure joy.

# GETTING TO KNOW YOU

**Materials Needed**
pen & paper

**Time Required**
20 minutes

**In The End**
Child will create an "assignment" for his grandparent to complete and send back to him

**Y**our child and his grandparent probably think that they know each other fairly well. But does your child know his grandparent's favorite color? His favorite artist? Let him create an "assignment" for his grandparent to do which will answer some of the questions he has.

On a sheet of notebook paper, have your child list several categories. He should then compose a question for the grandparent. Ask questions on each subject that will spark creativity and evoke enlightening responses from the grandparent.

For example:

- **History** – Who was your favorite president and why?

## OTHER IDEAS

Make a copy of the assignment and have your child complete it. Send it to your child's grandparent so he can learn more about his grandchild.

- **Geography** – What is your favorite state and why?

- **Math** – How many years older than me are you?

- **Reading** – What is your favorite book? What is it about?

- **Art** – Who is your favorite artist? Why?

- **Music** – If you were a musical instrument, which one would you be? Why?

- **Science** – If you were an animal, which animal would you be? Why?

After writing out the questions, send them to your child's grandparent with instructions to answer the questions and send the answers back to your child, who will enjoy learning about his grandparent.

# THINKING OF YOU

● ● ● ● ● ● ● ● ● ● ● ● ● ● ● ● ● ● ● ● ● ●

**Materials Needed**
pen & paper
**Time Required**
15 minutes
**In The End**
Child will send a letter to his grandparent sharing his thoughts and feelings

**O**ften it is the smallest, most seemingly insignificant things in our day that can cause us to remember somebody or think fondly of a certain memory.

Ask your child what it is that makes him think of his grandparent. It may be hearing a certain song that he remembers his grandparent singing or seeing a television show he thinks his grandparent would like. Perhaps it is eating an ice cream sundae like the one he shared with his grandparent on their last visit. It could be an animal, place, movie or rain shower that sparks his memory.

Whatever it is, encourage your child to write it down the next time he thinks of his grandparent. Have him explain just what it was which triggered the memory. He can draw a picture of it if he desires to do so.

Put the note in the mail to the child's grandparent, and it will certainly cause a smile. What grandparent wouldn't love to open his mailbox and get to read about how he was thought of by his special grandchild!

## OTHER IDEAS

To spark memories, find a photo of your child's grandparent and put it in a frame in your child's room.

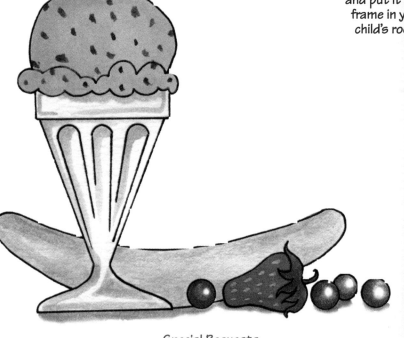